execution

>> create the vision
>> implement the plan
>> get the job done

Tom Gorman

Adams Media
Avon, Massachusetts

Published by Adams Business, an imprint of Adams Media, an F+W Publications
Company, 57 Littlefield Street, Avon, MA 02322
www.adamsmedia.com

ISBN 10: 1-59869-118-X
ISBN 13: 978-1-59869-118-4

Printed in Canada.

J   I   H   G   F   E   D   C   B   A

Library of Congress Cataloging-in-Publication Data
Gorman, Tom.
  Execution / Tom Gorman.
     p. cm.
  Includes index.
  ISBN-13: 978-1-59869-118-4 (pbk.)
  ISBN-10: 1-59869-118-X (pbk.)
  1. Management. 2. Business planning. I. Title.
  HD31.G67 2007
  658—dc22   2007018987

This publication is designed to provide accurate and authoritative information with
regard to the subject matter covered. It is sold with the understanding that the publisher is not engaged in rendering legal, accounting, or other professional advice. If
legal advice or other expert assistance is required, the services of a competent professional person should be sought.
   —From a *Declaration of Principles* jointly adopted by a Committee of the American
                        Bar Association and a Committee of Publishers and Associations

Many of the designations used by manufacturers and sellers to distinguish their product are claimed as trademarks. Where those designations appear in this book and
Adams Media was aware of a trademark claim, the designations have been printed
with initial capital letters.

This book is available at quantity discounts for bulk purchases.
For information, please call 1-800-289-0963.

contents

MANAGING GROWTH, SETBACKS, AND SUCCESS

introduction

The Way to Get Things Done

Execution. Productivity. Results. Accomplishments. These are the outcomes of good, solid management. Management is the art and science of getting things done through other people, and that's what this book is about. It's about managing people, money, processes, and resources whether you are in a company, a nonprofit organization, or on your own.

That's why we call it execution. It's not really about management in the Big Company sense of the term— you know, going to meetings, playing politics, having lunch, and so on. Execution is about getting things done. If you work in management in a large organization, or want to, you will benefit more by being able to execute than you will by sitting through meetings, playing politics, and all of that. That's because the key skill in any job today is getting the job done (although you'll probably still have to sit through meetings).

There are certain ways to go about getting the job done, regardless of the job. Getting the job done involves decision making, planning, scheduling, organizing people and resources, managing money, moving things forward, and controlling quality, among other tasks and skills. These tasks and skills are generic in the sense that there are proven ways to go about these activities that work in virtually any setting and situation.

Those are the skills you will learn in this book, which will enable you to execute—to get things done through other people or on your own. Sometimes the people you will need to get things done through won't actually be on your staff. In today's world of lean organizations, entrepreneurial start-ups, and virtual working arrangements, people may work as full-time, part-time, or temporary employees, or as indepen-dent contractors or freelancers. They may know more about what they do than you ever will, and they may even be smarter than you in some ways.

That's okay. In real life, execution rarely works the way it does in movies. In the movies, an executive (someone who executes the organization's plans) tells subordinates what to do, and they do it. Meanwhile, in real life, people may or may not report to the executive, probably won't just follow orders, and will always need more in the way of direction than someone yelling, "Just get it done!" Also, unlike the movies, you can't go around asking, "Why am I surrounded by idiots?"—or pulling guns on people for that matter. In real life you must know how to execute plans, not people.

Executive Skills

Other key business and life skills are covered in other books in this Adams Media series, such as *Innovation*,

Persuasion , and *Motivation*. Here in *Execution*, we deal with the nuts and bolts of getting things done. Here you will learn methods, skills, and tools of decision making, planning, goal setting, scheduling, budgeting, follow-up, and quality control. You will also learn how to manage yourself, and how to understand and solve problems that inevitably occur when you try to get something done.

This book is organized into three parts:

Part 1: Managing Plans and People shows how to define and communicate goals and ways of reaching them, and explains the functions of a business—even a one-person business—and how to set them up. It also shows how to set yourself up for success by managing your time well and getting help when you need it.

Part 2: Managing Money, Projects, and Processes reveals the basics of budgeting and finance, and shows how to go about public relations and marketing, which are becoming key to success in almost any endeavor. This part also covers proven decision-making and project management tools.

Part 3: Managing Growth, Setbacks, and Success shows how to grow a project or a business into something that can sustain itself—and your ambitions—and how to identify and deal with troubleshooting as opposed to problem solving.

This book recognizes that business and all other forms of organizational life have evolved and are continuing to evolve. Therefore the formula for success, and for getting things done, has evolved. But certain tools, methods, and frameworks, such as profit and loss, cause and effect, and planning and execution always apply. They just need to be updated from time to time.

Who Am I?

I've been a middle-manager in divisions of two *Fortune* 500 companies and, for the past ten years, have been a full-time freelance business writer focused mainly on books that I write under my own name and for clients who require ghostwriting and editorial services. I also hold an MBA from New York University's Leonard N. Stern School of Business.

As a corporate manager I was fortunate to work for some excellent senior managers, as well as a few who could be described as "negative role models"—managers who taught me what not to do. I held a variety of positions in marketing and product management, including director of product development in one company and director of publication services for a $50 million consulting firm. So I've managed people in project-oriented situations, which have a beginning, middle, and end, and in process-oriented situations, which never end because you continually produce the same product or service for customers or for stakeholders within the company.

Both as a corporate manager and out on my own, I have employed independent contractors and freelancers. So I am deeply familiar with the practice of managing by influence and teambuilding as opposed to issuing orders. Indeed, influence almost always works better than orders, especially when you are getting things done through intelligent people exercising specialized skills of their own.

And that, of course, is what execution is all about: getting things done through other people, while managing yourself toward success.

Are you ready to start?

MANAGING PLANS
AND PEOPLE

part 1

" DON'T AGONIZE. **ORGANIZE**. "

—Florynce Kennedy
(social activist)

1

Execution: The Way to Get Things Done

Getting things done—whether you're doing them yourself or getting them done through others as a manager or as an entrepreneur—calls for organization. I don't mean being organized in the clean-desk versus messy-desk sense of the term, though many of us might do better in a more orderly working environment. I'm talking about being organized in another sense.

Execution calls for organizing your thoughts, actions, time, and resources for efficiency and effectiveness. Efficiency means that you are getting things done with the right amounts of effort, time, and resources. Effectiveness means that you are getting the job done properly and reaching your intended goals.

In this chapter we look at the overall issue of execution and how to go about it. We'll touch upon the goals and results that you may want or need to achieve, and at the general ways to think about those goals, results, and means of execution.

Basic Background

To work in an effective and efficient manner, you should understand three basic concepts: cause and effect; risk and reward; and goals and success. You may think you understand these concepts, but a good look around you and perhaps at situations in your own life may reveal that they can easily be misunderstood or misapplied.

These three concepts form the environment in which execution takes place. Cause and effect links your actions to the results you generate. Risk and reward links the element of probability to the results you may (or may not) generate. Goals and success link your state of mind to the results you create.

Such linkages help you develop a framework for setting goals, planning your actions, allocating your time and other resources, and evaluating your progress.

ef•fect

1. noun: result of doing or not doing something, as in "The effect of lower prices will be more customers."

2. verb: to bring about a result, as in "To effect higher sales, we cut our prices."

Cause and Effect

We live in a world of cause and effect. Every action we take generates a result. Some of these results are the exact ones we want. Others are not the ones we want. But often we create results without giving much thought to what we want, and that's too bad.

However, the latter fact presents a huge opportunity because creating results that you've given no thought to may amount to a waste of energy. For instance, many of us spend hours browsing the Web, watching television, or working on minute details of our jobs without really thinking about what we're getting out of it. If we're enjoying it or accomplishing something, that's fine. If we're not, however, we may be missing real opportunities to enjoy ourselves or accomplish things.

> Organizing is what you do before you do something, so that when you do it, it is not all mixed up.
> —A. A. Milne (author)

The results we create are the effects of our actions. What kind of effects do I mean? Broadly, our actions affect the physical world, other people, and ourselves.

We affect the physical world when we build or maintain a thing or place, or destroy or neglect it. If we plant dune grass on a beach or lakeshore, we'll probably preserve it from erosion. If we maintain our cars, they'll run better and last longer. On the other hand, if we destroy a sand dune we may foster erosion. If we neglect auto maintenance, our cars won't run well or last long.

af•fect

1. noun: behavior, as in "The customer's affect was quite belligerent."

2. verb: to influence something, as in "We can affect sales by changing our prices."

We affect others in our interactions with them. An interaction can be anything from a pleasant remark while you're buying a pack of gum to a major argument over a matter of policy at work. Usually, we affect others in small ways, but those small effects can add up to major ones. If you've ever described someone as "happy-go-lucky" or "a pill" you know

Take Action
See the book *Motiva-tion* in this Adams Media series to learn how to get yourself charged up about improving your habits and behavior.

what I mean. That impression results from the positive or negative effects they've created in their interactions with you and others. We affect other people by the way we dress, drive, talk to them, look at them, and listen to them. Even the way we think about people may affect them by affecting the way we treat them, sometimes without our knowing it.

Our actions have very definite effects on ourselves. The way we eat and exercise affects our health and fitness. The way we spend our time and money affects our success and finances. The books and newspapers we read, the movies and TV shows we watch, and the music we listen to all affect us. There's now a well-established connection between our habits and behavior and our levels of health, wealth, and happiness.

At the action level—at the level of execution—we definitely live in a world of cause and effect.

Risk and Reward

Considering risk and reward helps you deal with the uncertainties surrounding execution. Although the world operates on cause and effect, a wide range of effects can result from any given decision or action. For instance, saving and investing will, over time, generally cause wealth to accumulate. However, unforeseen events can affect the value of an investment. Therefore, risk is an element in any investment decision. Risk also attends most career, hiring, purchase, and personal decisions.

There are also unintended consequences. It's impossible to foresee every potential outcome, effect, and side effect of any but the simplest decisions or actions. For example, seat belts keep accident victims from hitting dashboards and windshields, but they also trap some of them in burning or submerged vehicles. (The latter cases, however, represent a miniscule number compared to those saved from injury by seatbelts.)

Characteristics of Risks and Rewards

A risk or a reward may be long term or short term, large or small. People who deal with risk for a living recognize many different types of risk. For instance, financial professionals think in terms of inflation risk, credit risk, and foreign-exchange risk, among others. Similarly, you will face a range of risks when you make decisions and execute plans for your employer or your own business, including:

Risk of failure: the possibility that you will fail to execute properly, or that you will execute properly and still fail to achieve the goal

Business risk: the possibility that your organization's growth, competitive position, or regulatory or legal status will be jeopardized

Financial risk: the possibility that you will lose invested money or make less money than you could have made from alternative pursuits

Professional risk: the possibility that a decision will hamper your career progress or tarnish your reputation

Emotional risk: the possibility that you will feel fear, anger, anxiety, or regret

Creative risk: the possibility that you will waste time, energy, and good will on a fruitless endeavor, or that your creation will fail to express what you wanted it to

People—sane business people anyway—don't take risks for their amusement. They risk money, time, resources, competitive position, and emotional turmoil with the expectation of a reward and a return. The potential rewards relate to prudently considered risks as follows:

- *Risk of failure provides the opportunity to make decisions, set goals, and execute plans as you see fit.*

- *Business risks offer the chance of more rapid growth, higher sales, or improved competitive position.*

- *Financial risks provide the opportunity for increased sales, profits, or income.*

- *Professional risks attend attempts to achieve advancement, extend your reputation, or increase your professional standing.*

- *Emotional risks hold the possibility of personal growth, deeper relationships, and increased happiness.*

- *Creative risks typically accompany true breakthroughs in business, artistic, and personal endeavors.*

Dealing with risk effectively in making decisions, setting goals, and executing plans involves assessing the risks and potential returns, and then managing the risks. At least some risk is inherent in virtually any decision or plan you make, and you can identify and manage most of those risks.

Goals and Success

Every decision and plan has a goal. You make a decision to achieve or create something and, in doing so, set a goal. Then you must create and execute the plan to reach that goal. So the first step in creating a plan is to identify the goal. Your plan must move you toward your goal in order to be worth executing in the first place.

Reaching a goal and achieving success, however, may be two different things. You must define the goal in a way that achieves the deeper objective of succeeding in your larger endeavor or purpose. For instance, the goal of increasing sales can be achieved in many ways, including negative ones. You can engage in price gouging, sell things to people who don't need them, or make false claims for your product or service. This would achieve the goal of increasing sales—in

price gou•ging

1. raising prices to exorbitant levels when customers have no alternative sources

2. practice that often occurs with essential products during emergencies or shortages

the short term. In the long term, however, you will lose business.

To succeed you must define your goals in ways that are in keeping with your values and your overall definition of success. It's useful to give your values and your definition of success some thought. This may involve some soul searching, but if you're old enough to be reading this, your values are probably formed and you probably have a comfort zone. But you may still have to think about your definition of success.

Another important aspect of goals and success is managing expectations, including your own. When you define a goal in truly ambitious terms, you may motivate yourself and others to exert great effort and achieve great things. However, be sure that you and everyone else understand that this is a "stretch" goal. Otherwise, you may define success unrealistically or too narrowly. In other words, when you define your goal, you define success—and failure. So define your goal with an eye toward what's motivational, achievable, and valuable.

Managers Manage

The activity and profession of management is generally defined as the art and science of getting things done through others. Here's how this definition breaks down.

Happy Successes?

I once heard a fellow say of another businessman, "He's very successful, but he's not happy." He was going through his second divorce and experiencing stress-related problems. Does that sound like success? Of course, the fellow meant financial success, but there are other measures of success. Your happiness, and that of those around you, should probably factor into your definition of success.

The "activity" of management encompasses all the tasks that managers perform. These include goal setting, planning, delegating, decision making, controlling, and other tasks that I'll cover in Chapter 2.

The "profession of management" began in the early part of the last century when the production of products moved from piecework to assembly lines. Professional management began in earnest when people applied scientific techniques, such as observation and analysis of working patterns and precise measurement of production, to workers' efforts. As you'll see in Chapter 8, scientific methods are still being used to improve production and quality.

Management is a profession because real

> **piecework**
>
> 1. production method in which each worker produces the entire item for sale
>
> 2. arrangement in which an employee is paid for the number of pieces produced

Boss or Manager?

Your manager is your boss, but a boss is not always a manager. A boss gets things done mainly by deciding what people should do and directing them to do it. A manager generally decides what results people should produce and guides them to produce them. Managers tend to tell people what to achieve, leaving the means of achievement more to them. However, managers, like bosses, occasionally need to give orders.

managers hold to certain principles and practices that produce results in virtually any environment. In other words, a manager in an automobile plant and a manager in a bank will tend to use the same principles and practices, which I cover in Chapter 2, despite their very different working environments.

The "art and science of getting things done through others" recognizes the human factor as well as the more mechanistic aspect of management. It's an art because good managers form and foster productive relationships with subordinates, superiors, and colleagues. They also use their experience, intuition, and emotions in their work as much as they use "scientific" methods of observing, measuring, and analyzing productive processes and levels of production. Let me emphasize that management means getting things done through others. I've heard many a worker decry the fact that managers don't do any work. Well, they do work. It's just not the same kind of work that workers do. Managers who do the work of their subordinates are not actually managing.

Entrepreneurs Organize

In this book I use the term "manager" generally to mean a manager in an established organization and "entrepreneur" to mean a manager in a start-up or growing business. To avoid repeating "managers and entrepreneurs" I'll often just say managers to mean both, but there is a distinction. Both managers and entrepreneurs have to execute, but entrepreneurs go about it in a different atmosphere, usually one with fewer resources and less bureaucracy than that in which managers operate. An entrepreneur must be a manager, but not every manager is, or should be, an entrepreneur.

The job of the entrepreneur is to organize what economists call the factors of production. Traditionally the factors of production are people, materials, and capital. Capital here means equipment, although many people take it to mean money, for obvious reasons.

My point, however, is that entrepreneurs play a very specific role in a capitalist economy. Someone has to get things organized if products are going to

> Businesses are made by people. We've proven time and time again that you can have a wonderful shop, and put a bloke in there who's no good, and he'll stuff it up. Put a good bloke in, and it just turns around like that.
> —Gerry Harvey (Australian entrepreneur)

ad·min·is·tra·tion

1. formal or official tasks, often small, that must be performed in an organization

2. gathering information, completing forms, maintaining files, and so on

3. also known as "admin"

be produced and services are going to be delivered. Resources, including people, don't organize themselves.

Once resources are organized, the entrepreneur becomes something of an evangelist for his product, service, and business. He leads his team on a mission to win customers, deliver a quality product, and grow into an established, successful business. Once that happens, the entrepreneur must become more of a manager. He has to learn to rely less on charisma and a sense of mission and more on controlling the resources and dealing with what many entrepreneurs see as more mundane details.

Many of these details are dull compared to forging the raw factors of production into a business. But customers, employees, and government agencies expect mundane details to be addressed when a business gets beyond the start-up stage and starts to grow. Customers want consistent quality, employees want professional management, and government agencies want the proper paperwork.

Administrative tasks of the latter type can be discouraging, especially in a one-person business. But they have to be performed, or you can face legal exposure, financial loss, or both. For instance, if you don't have insurance and your business is burglarized or damaged (say by water from a broken pipe upstairs), you might not be covered. If you don't pay your estimated quarterly incomes taxes, you'll pay more at the end of the year. Dealing with details like these, or making sure that someone else is dealing with them, is another key aspect of execution.

More Factors of Production

When you think about execution and the factors of production, it's best to broaden your thinking beyond the economist's traditional definition to include all the resources you'll need to implement your plan and achieve your goal. These include:

People: You need people for their skills, of course, but you also need their energy, enthusiasm, and commitment. Obtaining those elements calls for consciously selecting people for their energy, enthusiasm, and commitment, as well as for their skills.

Time: Time is so important that Chapter 4 covers use of this resource in depth. Scheduling and controlling your time, and often others' time, are essential execution skills.

Equipment and Materials: No organization can survive, let alone prosper, without obtaining the right equipment and materials for the tasks it must accomplish at the right price and on the right terms.

Information: Today, most professionals and organizations recognize information as a resource in its own right. You must have ways of capturing, accessing, analyzing, and understanding the information that you need in order to make sound decisions and execute your plans.

Money: This essential resource has become amazingly fluid, moving quickly toward opportunities to, well, make money. Indeed, the ability to make money with a product, service, business, or media creation has become the key to attracting investment funds. Of course, this has always been true, but today creative ideas—rather than the ability to build a factory and pump out a product—drive a tremendous amount of investment, particularly in the United States. However, you not only need a great idea, but you must also make it a reality, which calls for superb execution.

Managers and entrepreneurs organize these factors of production and direct them, by setting goals, making plans, and designing jobs so that the workers—meaning ordinary humans working reasonable hours—can do something useful and make money in the process. That is the role of management and it's an extremely important one. I'll talk about the ways in which managers do all of this, and the means they use to do it, in Chapter 2.

Can you Execute?

Execution ultimately depends on your ability to get things done, usually through other people. To be sure, you can accomplish a lot through your own efforts. But to magnify your efforts, and expand the scale of your ideas and endeavors, you must learn to organize and manage resources, including the skills of other people. That starts with learning the principles and practices of management.

> **PRACTICE GOLDEN RULE 1 OF MANAGEMENT** IN EVERYTHING YOU DO. MANAGE OTHERS THE WAY YOU WOULD LIKE TO BE MANAGED.
>
> —Brian Tracy
> (author)

2 Managing People: Principles and Practices

A manager differs from a boss in that a manager subscribes to certain principles and practices that define how professional managers do their jobs. There are, of course, some very good "bosses"—informally taught or self-taught managers—who might not be able to explain these principles and practices. They are typically quite bright and have a real talent for interpersonal relations and business decisions. Some of them are just "naturals."

Yet most of us benefit from knowledge and skill development when it comes to managing people, projects, and organizations. In fact, many of those naturals could learn a thing or two as well. Nobody's perfect.

> Research indicates that workers have three prime needs: interesting work, recognition for doing a good job, and being let in on things that are going on in the company.
> —Zig Ziglar (motivational speaker)

In this chapter we examine management principles and practices and how they operate at the action level. These principles and practices apply to virtually any professional or business situation in which you must get results through others, execute a project, or run an organization.

What Are Principles and Practices?

Management principles and practices are guidelines and methods that managers employ in their work. While there is some overlap, in general the principles are more conceptual while the practices are actions.

Broadly, the key management principles include:

- *Authority*

- *Responsibility*

- *Accountability*

- *Chain of command*

- *Span of control*

Authority: To be obeyed and respected, authority—that is, power—in an organization or a society must be legitimate. In a business, management's authority comes from the owners, which makes it legitimate. Unless they work in the business, the owners delegate their authority over the organization to managers and employees so the company's work can be done. For instance, in a corporation the shareholders delegate their authority to the board of directors, who delegate their authority to senior managers, who delegate their authority to middle managers, and so on. (Delegation is one of the practices covered later in this chapter.)

Having the authority to do something in an organization means that you have the power to do it. If you have purchasing authority up to $1,000, you have the power to authorize purchases up to that amount. To make a purchase of a higher amount, you need someone else's authorization. If you have hiring authority for a department, you have the power to hire people in that area.

Responsibility: A manager's or employee's responsibility is the function, area, and work that he or she oversees and controls, and is accountable for. What you think of as your job is your responsibility (or "area of responsibility"). Your responsibility also includes the standards for properly executing the related functions, tasks, and so on. For instance, the accounting function includes responsibility for tracking expenditures. The tasks might include verifying and maintaining records of purchases, and the standards could include accuracy and timeliness. Also, if you have people reporting to you, those subordinates are your responsibility.

Authority and Accountability

Problems occur when people are held accountable for responsibilities that they did not have enough authority to execute properly. A manager or employee can get the job done only if they have the power to get it done. People need the power to spend the money, hire the talent, and tap the resources needed to do the job they're charged with doing. Otherwise, it's unfair to hold them accountable for it.

Accountability: When managers and employees are given responsibility for tasks and goals, they must be held accountable for executing those tasks and achieving those goals. If they succeed, they should be rewarded; if they do not, they should not be rewarded or should experience negative consequences. Being held accountable means that there are positive and negative outcomes associated with excellent and poor performance. In that way it differs from responsibility, which merely defines what someone is accountable for.

Chain of Command: A military term, the chain of command calls for managers to give directives through the company hierarchy in an orderly way. Thus, the vice president of finance gives directives to financial analysts, not to the salespeople; the sales manager directs the salespeople and not the financial analysts. You disrespect the chain of command if you go over your boss's head and ask his boss for something he would probably refuse.

Span of Control: A manager must have the right sized function or set of responsibilities. If it's too large, she won't be able to manage it well. If it's too small, that is inefficient and may encourage micromanagement. In other words, managers need enough to keep busy but not enough to overwhelm them. They also need to manage functions that are related and that they understand.

mi•cro•man •age•ment

1. managing the details of subordinates' work rather than letting them do the work

2. inefficient and annoying use of a manager's time and energy

3. condition driven by some managers' personalities

The appropriate span of control also relates to the number of direct reports a manager has, that is, the number of subordinates who report directly to the manager. Too many, and the manager cannot manage them well; too few, and the manager may not have enough to do—although it's more common to have too many direct reports.

Practice These Practices

Again, management practices are things managers actually do. They are the tasks that managers perform in their roles as managers. Broadly, the key management practices include:

23

- *Decision making*

- *Planning*

- *Delegating*

- *Controlling*

- *Supporting*

Decision Making: The key issue facing any organization is what to do and how to do it. In a way, decision making could be considered an all-inclusive function. Every move a manager makes, including whether to have the salad or a hamburger for lunch, reflects a decision. But I'm talking about more profound and far-reaching decisions. In fact, they are so profound and far-reaching that I devote all of Chapter 7 to decision making.

Planning: This practice is another broadly inclusive one that also warrants its own chapter, which is Chapter 3, the next chapter. In a way, planning is half of management. It entails goal setting, defining the tasks and resources required to reach the goal, budgeting and scheduling, managing risks, and contingency planning.

Also, management must not only plan the actions and identify

con•tin•gen •cy plan

1. plan that goes into effect if conditions change or the original plan fails

2. also known as Plan B, although there can be multiple contingency plans

necessary resources, but also design the work. It is management's responsibility to organize work, systems, and resources so that ordinary people—meaning employees with the

> Good management consists of showing average people how to do the work of superior people.
> —**John D. Rockefeller (founder, Standard Oil)**

right level of skills, intelligence, and motivation—can achieve the goals. It is not the employees' responsibility to design their jobs.

Delegating: Proper delegation is a bit of an art. It calls for sound decision making and planning, and clear communication. You have to delegate tasks to the right people and in the right way. They need to know the goal, the means of achieving it, and the resources they need to achieve it. They also need to have the authority to get the job done. Poor communication stands as one of the major shortcomings in delegation for many managers. I'll discuss communication later in this chapter.

Controlling: Once you have a plan and have delegated the work, you have to monitor progress and make any corrections needed to keep the plan on budget, on schedule, and on course. Formally known as "controlling to plan" and informally as "follow up," this practice is a key component of management that's often overlooked. That is, people often plan, but then don't refer to the plan when they are executing it.

Let Them Do It

To delegate well, understand that your subordinate won't do the job the way you would, but can still do a good job. It took me awhile to realize this. Early on in my management career, I would edit subordinates' written work far too heavily. Why? Because they weren't writing the way I would write. I was allocating my time badly and turning them off to writing, and to my management style.

Supporting: Recall that bosses, as opposed to managers, revel in "telling people what to do." Their idea of supporting people often runs along the lines of yelling, "Just get it done," or "What don't you understand about that?" A big part of a real manager's role is coaching people toward better performance, teaching them or exposing them to new skills, and mentoring them so they can move to larger responsibilities. This takes skill and effort.

Communication: The Essential Skill

Most aspects of a manager's job involve communication. If you have subordinates or deal with independent contractors in your own business, you will spend a good portion of your time communicating with them in various modes. These modes will probably include setting goals, planning, delegating, coaching, mentoring, reprimanding, and praising.

Communication skills are cited so often as a key management skill that it's become something of a cliché or code for "BS artist." If you intend to get things done through other people, you must be able to communicate clearly and persuasively. This includes written as well as verbal communication.

Listening skills are the starting point in good communication. So few people encounter people who actually listen to them, with full attention and without interrupting, that many find it somewhat odd. It's almost natural for most of us to use the time when someone is talking to think about whether we agree and how we'll respond. Instead, listen and try to grasp the other person's perspective, feelings, and understanding of the situation.

This means listening with an open mind. Most of us are barely aware of our assumptions, preconceptions, and prejudices about other people. We're also unaware that we project our own feelings, fantasies, or foibles onto them, or respond to certain things in habitual

> **frame of ref•er•ence**
>
> 1. facts, ideas, concerns, and assumptions that feed into a person's point of view
>
> 2. common understanding that two or more people can share

ways. The truth is that while we are all the same in essential ways, we also differ in the particulars, especially in the way we comprehend a situation. So be sure that you clearly comprehend other people and their understanding of whatever is at hand.

Over time, listening and the understanding that it fosters promotes trust and a shared frame of reference between people. That trust becomes the context for communication in which there's a good chance that the message sent by the speaker is the one received by the listener as those roles alternate during the interchange.

How to Talk

Although most of us have more practice at it than we do at listening, talking is also, of course, important to communication. In business, you'll generally get the best results by speaking directly in concrete language. However, being too direct can alienate people. In other words, don't give orders, or if you must give orders, don't issue them brusquely. Yet be precise so that people know what you expect. Here are some examples of vague and precise language in some common business situations. The statements are from

Points of View

Police officers routinely encounter wildly varying accounts of accidents or crimes from eyewitnesses. Why? Because everyone interprets what they see and hear—a situation, an event, other people—differently. You will often hear the movie *Rashomon*, from the great Japanese director Akira Kurosawa, invoked to describe this phenomenon. The movie concerns the differing accounts of a crime from four people.

a manager to a subordinate, and in general the more precise ones will get better results.

Too Vague	More Precise
I'd like you to turn this around quickly.	I'd like you to complete this project by noon next Monday.
Please get in touch with somebody about that.	Please e-mail Peter in Finance about those missing pages.
I can't talk now. Please grab me some other time.	I'm sorry I'm too busy to talk now. Please come back after four o'clock.

A lot of communication from managers aims to assist subordinates in getting their work done on time and up to standards. Vague language creates misunderstanding about what is expected and when it's expected. But, again, being a manager and speaking precisely doesn't mean bossing people around. Good communicators see their subordinates and their superiors as colleagues all focused on getting the job done properly.

Indeed, it's a good idea to cultivate an objective attitude toward people on the job. Think of them as you would fellow players on a team. You want to work together toward

Take Action
If you're serious about a management career, particularly in a large organization, read the work of Peter F. Drucker, arguably the first "business guru." A good starting point is a paperback compilation of his writing called *The Essential Drucker* (Harper Business, 2003).

Take Action
For resources on management, some free and some available only to members, visit *www.ama net.org,* the Web site of the American Management Association.

common goals. It's more important to respect one another and work well together than to become friends, which often happens too.

Finally, share information with your employees to the greatest extent possible. Most employees resent being uninformed, especially about developments that affect them. While you can't usually tell every employee everything you know and cannot compromise others' privacy, you should keep your people informed about anything that directly affects them.

Best Practices

Over the past several years the term "best practices" has become popular. It refers to ways of doing things in specific areas of business that have been more or less accepted as the best way of going about something. Often, best practices emerge from the way that highly successful companies have gone about things.

For example, one of the goals in manufacturing is to ensure that suppliers provide materials, parts, and components of a certain level of quality. Related best practices might include showing your suppliers your production facility and processes so they see how you use their materials, developing detailed quality and performance specifications for them, and rewarding those who supply materials of the highest quality by giving them more of your business.

Best practices have been defined across all industries—where they're also known as industry standards or industry best practices—and in all functions; for instance, there are best accounting practices, best hiring practices, and so on. Best practices must often be updated because of human ingenuity, changing market or economic conditions, and new technologies.

Often a company will hire a consulting firm to identify best practices in its industry. The consultants will research domestic and foreign competitors' operations and help the company adopt or adapt those practices for its operation. Not all best practices can be used by every company. Some companies are constrained by their small (or large) size, limited resources, bureaucracy, or lack of motivation or imagination. But every manager should understand best practices in his function and industry, and apply them to the extent possible.

To Curse (and Praise) Management Fads

As an author and ghostwriter of business books and as a corporate survivor, I'm quite familiar with management fads. They are fairly easy to identify because newspapers, magazines, and, yes, books prominently feature the fad for a period of months or even years. Good examples of what I consider fads include empowerment, diversity, leadership, and customer-focus.

Don't get me wrong. I'm not against these things. I consider them fads because many—though not all—

31

management teams tend to pay lip service to them for awhile, and then forget about them. All too often words like "empowerment," "diversity," and "leadership" are just ideas—slogans, actually—rather than methods. To empower employees, achieve diversity, exercise leadership, or focus on customers, you need a method and real management commitment.

A good look at major companies and financial institutions reveals that certain interests of management do amount to fads. How can the heads of major organizations say they're empowering employees when workers can be laid off at will? That's powerlessness, not empowerment. How can managers say they support diversity when they still talk about "tolerating" differences? Tolerating implies putting up with differences, not embracing them. How can they say they are leaders when they hog company profits in the form of huge salaries? Growth in CEO compensation has far outstripped growth in employee compensation. How can they say their companies focus on customers, when service is so bad that the phrase "Your call is important to us" is a national joke and the title of a book? You have to take care of customers, not just say you are customer-focused.

EARMARKS OF A MANAGE MENT FAD

- More talk than action

- Slogans instead of methods

- Flavor-of-the-month syndrome

- Lots of excitement, but not much funding

Real Issues in Management

Not everything that we may think of as a management fad is a fad. Neither is all that management treats as a fad actually a fad. Indeed, management priorities in business change as the challenges and conditions that organizations face change. This gives rise to energetic efforts to address issues as well as to management fads. That is to say, achieving diversity, focusing on customers, operating ethically, and balancing work and family life are issues that many companies take seriously rather than treat as fads.

"

DEVELOPING THE PLAN IS ACTUALLY LAYING OUT THE SEQUENCE OF EVENTS THAT HAVE TO OCCUR FOR YOU TO ACHIEVE YOUR GOAL.

"

—George L. Morrisey (author and management consultant)

3

Planning Precedes Execution

As discussed in Chapter 2, part of a manager's job is to set goals and develop plans to reach them. With clear goals, you and your team know what you are working toward and why. With solid plans you stand an excellent chance of reaching your goals. Without goals and plans you have no chance of success.

In this chapter we examine the basics of goal setting and planning, as well as several tools for planning. These are standard tools that enable you to chart a course to your objective and understand what it will take to get you there. That way, you can develop a plan you can execute with confidence.

Many people think they are planning when they mull things over endlessly in their heads. Planning, which is the act of bringing

PLANS MUST CONSIDER

- Goals and tasks
- People and skills
- Time and money
- Materials and equipment

the future into the present so that you can influence the future, should take place on paper.

Written plans will be more precise, more "real," and will constitute a record so people can be held accountable for executing their parts of the plan. Also, once a plan is written, you can return to it and adjust it if that becomes necessary.

Take Action
To learn more about planning tools, and other good general management information, visit *www .mindtools.com.*

Goal to Go

The goals you choose define the result that you intend to create. They also affect the amount of time, money, skill, effort, and resources you'll need. Choose the wrong goal, and you will waste some of those things. You can damage your organization or your professional or personal life with the wrong goals—so choose goals wisely.

Goals can be stated in various ways, but to be of use the stated goal must have four characteristics. It must be specific, measurable, time limited, and achievable.

Specific

A goal must be specific because you have to know what you are trying to create in order to create it. One definition of the creative process is keeping the picture of what you want to create firmly in mind and then shaping the medium and materials—your film, painting, business, or life—to that picture. The clearer the picture of the goal, the better you can see the gap between the reality and the goal and the more accurately you can shape reality to the goal. Note, however, that the picture in your head may be perfect, and the reality, with all its imperfections, may never truly match the picture.

In more mundane terms, you can't hit a target that you can't see. So the target should be described in precise terms. For instance, saying that you want to be the biggest business in your industry might not be a precise enough, or even useful, goal. What if every other outfit becomes smaller and you fail to grow? That may not make your business what you want it to be. Nor are words like "the best" or "the highest quality" terribly useful, unless those things can be objectively measured.

Measurable

A goal becomes measurable when you quantify it. Quantitative measures enable you to assess your progress and achievement in objective terms. For instance, many companies target specific growth rates, such as growing sales by at least 20 percent annually or doubling the number of customers buying more than $5,000 of goods and services a year. Another useful measure would be market share of a specific prod-

mar•ket share

1. company's percentage of the total industry sales of a product or service in a geographic area or type of customer

2. example: First Bank of Omaha has a 28 percent share of new car loans in Nebraska

uct or service. Measurable professional goals would include being hired by a certain company or one of two or three companies, or being promoted to a certain position. Measurable personal goals would be to own a certain car or house, or to lose a certain amount of weight, by a certain date.

Whenever possible, express goals in dollars, percentages, growth rates, or other numerical values. Some goals cannot be measured numerically but can still be clear, for instance earning a certain degree or promotion by a certain time. That last element is key: to be really useful, the goal should include the element of time.

Time-Limited

Setting a deadline for reaching a goal kicks up your motivation and helps you define your timeline. One of the key tricks in any form of dramatic writing or filmmaking is to have a deadline. Dr. Evil gives world leaders a deadline, the bomb starts ticking, our hero is launched on his mission—and we pay attention.

Deadlines not only focus attention and direct energy, but they also help you set priorities and allocate time to tasks in the correct order. Plans usually call for completing certain tasks by certain dates. These interim deadlines, or milestones, help you measure progress toward the goal well before the final deadline.

Achievable

A goal should be achievable but ambitious. If a goal is impossible and you know it or suspect it, then you're kidding yourself. That may be okay, if it works for you. Some of us adopt impossible targets and figure that if we fall short, it will be no problem because we still made terrific strides. But to give other people unachievable goals may make them feel manipulated or discouraged. However, most people do their best when they're working toward ambitious goals, as explained in greater detail in the book *Motivation* in this Adams Media series.

The following are examples of specific, measurable, time-limited, and, hopefully, achievable goals:

Business goal: To open for business and be soliciting customers by June 30, and to land our first major account by September 1

Financial goal: To raise our net profit to 12 percent of sales in our next fiscal year

Marketing goal: To increase our share of the mattress market in Florida by 2 percent in each of the next five years

Operating goal: To move our production facilities to Alabama within three years

Professional goal: To earn the designation of Certified Financial Analyst within three years

Personal goal: To enter, run, and complete the Boston Marathon in two years

The Planning Process

Much of the success of any plan depends on the environment in which the plan was created and the purposes of the plan. In truth, some planning, particularly strategic planning in large outfits, is done for show or as an empty exercise. Such plans are founded on sloppy or wrongheaded assumptions about the achievability of goals, availability of resources, or required time. Or they are done to justify an unwise but preordained senior management decision.

Useful planning occurs in an atmosphere of honesty, open communication, reasonable goals, and few, if any, preconceived notions about how to achieve them. Useful plans usually result from the following practices:

Gathering the needed information: Planning must be done with solid information on the competitive, economic, and market environments, and on the available resources.

Involving the right people: Early in the process, managers and planners must involve the people who will **(a)** be responsible for achieving the results **(b)** do the actual work and **(c)** be affected by the plan. Collectively these people are called stakeholders, because they all have a stake in the plan and its outcome.

> Begin challenging your assumptions. Your assumptions are your windows on the world. Scrub them off every once in a while, or the light won't come in.
> —**Alan Alda (actor)**

Making conservative assumptions: A plan filled with rosy assump-

40

tions about the available time and resources isn't a plan—it's a wish list. One good method is to develop optimistic, pessimistic, and best-guess estimates for factors that can't be controlled, such as interest rates, economic growth, certain costs, and time.

Establishing responsibility and accountability: A staggering number of plans fail to clearly establish who will do what, by when, and to what standard. Often this occurs when "the team" is going to be responsible, and everyone takes that to mean that another team member will perform the task. This is often the case with unpleasant tasks. Every task must have someone, preferably one person or a lead person, responsible for doing it.

Two Major Types of Planning

In business you'll most often find yourself involved in strategic planning and project planning.

Strategic planning encompasses the entire organization and all its functions. In other words, each part of the organization plays a role in executing the plan. The overall goals break down into functional goals, interim

KEY REASONS THAT PLANS FAIL

- Unachievable goals or faulty assumptions

- No one assigned responsibilities and accountability

- Failure to control to plan during execution

goals, and tasks that functions, individuals, and teams must achieve, perform, and execute.

Project planning centers on a key function or area and a specialized goal. The goal may be to develop a new product, build a new facility, enter a new market, conduct a new research study, develop a new sales channel, or locate a new acquisition.

The Awful Truth

In my experience, strategic planning in large companies suffers from four flaws: First, it tends to be too top-down. Second, it focuses more on cutting costs than on growing the business. Third, the plans often assume resources that won't really be available. Fourth, the plans are rarely referred to again, except for the targets.

The distinction I usually make is that strategic plans (and business plans) apply to ongoing operations while project plans apply to, well, projects. Projects have a beginning, a middle, and an end, whereas the work of production, finance, accounting, marketing, sales, and customer service never end.

Strategic Planning

Strategic planning begins with one or more goals and a strategic assessment. The goals should be modified if the strategic assessment uncovers something that affects those goals either positively (a major competitor just went out of business) or negatively (a major competitor just entered your business).

STRATEGIC PLANNING TEMPLATE

The steps in formulating a strategic plan are to:

○ *Define the goals*

○ *Analyze the environment*

○ *Assess the resources*

○ *Identify the tasks, timeframes, and responsibilities*

○ *Execute the tasks and control to plan*

Define the Goals

The organization should have a large, motivating goal that will organize the thinking and activities of everyone in the outfit. The most common and widely accepted goal is to maximize long-term shareholder value, which means constantly improving the worth of the company to the owners. In that context, specific goals can include growing the market share, winning better customers, increasing prices, acquiring other businesses, or other growth strategies.

Analyze the Environment

Your plan will be executed in the real world, which means that you have to take the real world into account. This entails gathering information on anything that may affect your plan. Depending on the industry and organization, that may mean doing research on customers and prospects, competitors, emerging technologies, or economic conditions. It's best to survey customers directly, either formally or informally. However, you can gather information on competitors, technologies, and conditions from news accounts, conferences, and reports and newsletters from specialized publishers.

Having information is one thing, but you must often analyze it to understand its potential impact.

Assess Your Resources

You must assess your resources in the five major areas that I referred to more broadly in Chapter 2 as the factors of production: people and skills; equipment and materials; information; money; and time. You want to assess the resources you currently have available and those that you could tap. For example, a business has people on staff and the ability to hire more people, and money in the bank and some borrowing power.

The act of planning largely comes down to allocating your resources to the tasks that will produce the most return for the investment. I'll explain what that means in more detail in Chapter 8.

Identify Tasks, Timeframes, and Responsibilities

The tasks, of course, are those that will move you toward your goals, and the timeframes are periods and deadlines for performing those tasks. We'll discuss ways of planning tasks and timeframes in the section on project planning later in this chapter. This is critical because it represents your roadmap to execution in that the tasks, timeframes, and responsibilities define who does what and when they do it in order to execute the plan.

Execute the Tasks

Of course a plan is useless unless you execute it. A good plan will include frequent milestones to measure progress as well as indicators regarding the use of resources. The milestones are generally indicators that certain tasks are complete along with the dates for completion. Indicators such as budget and schedule variances will help you control to plan. I'll discuss budgets in Chapter 6.

Controlling schedules calls for, first, having reasonable estimates for how long tasks take. It's easy to be too optimistic and to find yourself behind schedule almost from the first week. The other key element is to constantly check your progress against the schedule, and if (or rather, when) you see tasks taking too long, find out why and take action. Possible actions might include getting more help, omitting or compressing certain tasks, accepting "good enough" as opposed to perfect, or, of course, revising the schedule. I am not, however, suggesting cutting corners if it undermines quality or, especially, safety.

Project Planning

Project planning entails tasks similar to those in strategic planning. As a discipline, project planning, focuses more heavily on tasks and scheduling, and again it usually focuses on a specific, time-limited effort in a defined function.

As noted at the start of this chapter, organizations, managers, engineers, researchers, and academics have developed various planning tools. They help you think clearly about the necessary tasks and the order in which they must be performed. In other words, they help you structure and schedule tasks. The key tools I'll explain here are the Critical Path Method (CPM), the Program Evaluation and Review Technique (PERT), and GANTT charts.

Critical Path Method (CPM)

The Critical Path Method, or CPM, is a visual tool for planning tasks. It was developed by the DuPont Corporation in the late 1950s for managing projects like the construction of huge production facilities. However, it also works for smaller projects with multiple, interdependent steps.

Let's say you're planning to open a restaurant and face the following major tasks:

Task Code	Task Description	Predecessors	Time (weeks)
A	Find location	none	4
B	Negotiate lease	A	1
C	Do renovations	A, B	5
D	Hire chef	none	4
E	Purchase fixtures	A, B	2
F	Plan menu	D	2
G	Hire and train crew	D, F	5
H	Install and test fixtures	A, B, E, F, G	2
I	Conduct a dry run	All	1

(Total time) 26 weeks

The first step is to define the necessary tasks and put them in order. Predecessor tasks are those that must be completed before others can begin. Then you estimate the time each task will consume. In real life, you would identify all the tasks, but to keep this simple, I've left out lining up advertising, purchasing food, and several others.

Connecting the Dots

The final step is to diagram the tasks as shown in the previous table. Once you see them laid out like this, you can more easily see which tasks can (and can't) be performed concurrently. For instance, in this restaurant example you might think of the whole project as having two tracks: a facilities track and a food track. The facilities track comprises the tasks that get the restaurant ready (A, B, C, and E), while the food track comprises those related to food preparation and presentation (D, F, and G).

Critical Path Chart

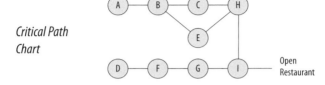

Critical Path Chart with Task Times (in Weeks)

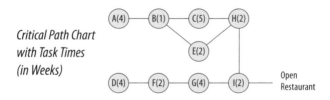

CPM helps you see how you may be able to collapse the project and finish it in less elapsed time than the total project will require. To do that you have to add the time for each task, which I show in the CPM chart in Figure 3-2.

Now, here's why this is called the Critical Path Method. This tool lets you identify the longest path through the project—and that is called the critical path. In our restaurant example, that path extends from point A to point I, and amounts to fourteen weeks. This means that the total elapsed time of the project will be fourteen weeks, even though the total time for the tasks is twenty-one weeks. The facilities track will take twelve weeks, but the nine-week food track can be completed concurrently. Of course, the food track and most of the facilities track must be complete before fixtures are tested, and all tasks must be completed before the dry run.

In fact, the food track can be collapsed from eighteen weeks to sixteen weeks by planning the menu with the chef while hiring the crew. This doesn't improve the total elapsed time, but there is no reason not to get done whatever you can in the most efficient way possible.

Program Evaluation and Review Technique (PERT)

PERT, which stands for Program Evaluation and Review Technique, resembles the Critical Path Method, but with a difference. PERT lets you make optimistic, pessimistic, and best-guess estimates of the time it will take to complete each task and the entire project. You calculate a weighted average by assigning a value of 1 to the pessimistic and optimistic estimates, and a value of 4 to the best guess. Then you plug the values into the following formula:

Take Action

If you'd like to explore project management software, you can find planning tools such as Critical Path Management and GANTT charts in project planning software packages such as Microsoft Project.

Estimated Time = (Optimistic $\times$ 1) + (Best Guess $\times$ 4) + (Pessimistic $\times$ 1) / 6

You divide by six because $1 + 4 + 1 = 6$, and you are calculating a weighted average of the time estimates. In a way you are saying that there is about a 66 percent probability (four chances in six) of achieving the best-guess schedule for a task, about a 17 percent chance of achieving the optimistic schedule, and a 17 percent chance of the pessimistic schedule.

Let's say the best-guess estimate of a task's duration is ten weeks, the pessimistic estimate is fourteen weeks, and the optimistic estimate is eight weeks. The PERT formula would calculate the estimated time as follows:

Estimated time $= 8 + (10 \times 4) + 14 / 6$

Estimated time $= 62 / 6$

Estimated time $= 10.3$ weeks

I am describing a simplified version of PERT. The actual system can incorporate very sophisticated statistical techniques. For our purposes, the value of PERT is really the optimistic and pessimistic estimates, which help you consider possible deviations from the best guess. In this case, since 10.3 is greater than 10, it's likely that any variance from the best guess would be in the pessimistic direction.

In my own version of PERT, I assign pessimistic estimates to large tasks that I can't directly control. Then I give my client or boss only the pessimistic estimates for these tasks, and thus the project. Still, it's often hard to be pessimistic enough. On a product-development project I worked on, I completed the project eight weeks later than my best guess, due to programming problems beyond my control. But it was only two weeks later than the pessimistic estimate, which was the one I had supplied to my boss. And I had doubled the programming time estimate that the management information systems department had given me!

GANTT Charts

The GANTT Chart functions somewhat like the Critical Path Method in that it enables you to schedule tasks concurrently and see the times for tasks and the elapsed time for the total project. The following chart presents the tasks for opening the restaurant in a GANTT chart.

Week	1	2	3	4	5	6	7	8	9	10	11	12	13	14
Task														
A	▓	▓	▓	▓										
B					▓									
C						▓	▓	▓	▓	▓				
D	▓	▓	▓											
E					▓									
F						▓								
G							▓	▓	▓	▓	▓			
H												▓	▓	
I														▓

**GANTT Chart for Restaurant
Project**

The GANTT chart lets you clearly
see when a task begins and ends and
the sequence in which tasks must be
done. Bear in mind that all tasks listed
in any of these planning tools must be
assigned to specific people who will be
responsible for them.

Scenario and Crisis Planning

Nowadays, no discussion of planning would be complete without considering scenario and crisis planning. Also known as "What if?" exercises, this type
of planning considers possibilities that may seem
remote, but which could have potentially devastating effects. In scenario planning, you imagine these
kinds of possibilities and develop a plan for addressing them. For example, you might include business
developments such as a new technology that could
make your product obsolete or a competitor being
purchased by a company that could outspend you
in marketing. Many companies anticipate events
such as floods, hurricanes, and other "acts of God"
as well as terrorist attacks, wars, epidemics, and
recessions.

Scenario planning or crisis planning usually points
up the need for contingency plans to address business or economic developments. These plans typically

call for backup systems in other geographical areas to deal with floods, hurricanes, terrorism, and other devastating events.

> Good fortune is what happens when opportunity meets with planning.
> —**Thomas Edison (inventor)**

On a more general level, scenario planning enables you to ask any "What if?" question and anticipate various outcomes and the most useful response you could launch. No one recommends spending a huge amount of time on scenario planning for a small business, but considering worst-case scenarios—as opposed to obsessing about them—can enable you to make some preparation and not find yourself totally at sea should the worst occur.

" **DON'T SAY YOU DON'T HAVE ENOUGH TIME**. YOU HAVE EXACTLY THE SAME NUMBER OF HOURS PER DAY THAT WERE GIVEN TO HELEN KELLER, PASTEUR, MICHELANGELO, MOTHER TERESA, LEONARDO DA VINCI, THOMAS JEFFERSON, AND ALBERT EINSTEIN. "

—H. Jackson Brown, Jr.
(author)

4 Managing Yourself: Using Your Time Wisely

You've heard the expression time is money. It's true, but more important, time is actually your life. How you choose to use your time each day amounts to the way you choose to spend your life. This, of course, assumes that you actually choose how to spend your time. Far too many of us either dash from task to task, giving little thought to their value, or drift through the day on autopilot, moving through a routine that has been set by others or produced by repetition.

Everyone gets twenty-four hours, (which is 1,440 minutes or 86,400 seconds) a day.

time man•age•ment

1. planning, allocating, and using time in effective, efficient, enjoyable ways

2. relating your use of time to your goals

3. set of skills that can be learned and practiced

How you use those hours, minutes, and seconds is the most important decision you face each day. This chapter will help you face and make that decision. It examines time management concepts and tasks, and a few tools that can help you make the most of your time.

Time and Execution

The relevance of time management to the skill of execution should be apparent. Time is a basic resource. If you use any resource to do the wrong things or to do the right things incorrectly, you have not effectively and efficiently moved toward your goal or created the desired result.

Conversely, if you have goals and a plan and you allocate the budgeted time to the tasks in the plan, you will make progress. Okay, I know it's not that simple. But the fact that it doesn't always work perfectly is no reason to forgo time management. Parachutes don't always open, but you'd be a fool to jump out of an airplane without one.

Take Action

For a different take on time management, especially if you like New Age approaches, pick up a copy of *The Tao of Time* by Diana Hunt and Pam Hait (Fireside, 1991).

Time management is a key personal and organizational skill. That is, the people in an organization must collectively spend their time doing the right things in the right way. Virtually any study of productivity involves evaluating the ways in which time is used. Indeed, the study of time usage goes back to the emerging days of the profession of management,

Efficiency Experts

In the early days of "scientific" management, large companies hired people known as efficiency experts. The scientific method calls for observation, measurement, and analysis, so these experts would watch workers perform tasks, time them, measure their production, and try to find ways to arrange the tasks to improve their performance. These folks have been spoofed in movies as white-coated, clipboard-equipped nerds, but their time-and-motion studies fostered professional management.

when efficiency experts structured production methods.

So, time is an essential, valuable resource for individuals and organizations, and it has to be managed as such.

Basic Tasks of Time Management

Sound time management depends on four basic tasks. In other words, if you fail to execute any one of these tasks, you may fail to reach your goals; if you do execute them, you stand a good chance of achieving your goals.

time-and-mo•tion stu•d•ies

1. research that measures workers' activities and production

2. studies that are still used in various forms in many organizations

1. You must have written goals and written plans for achieving them, including a schedule of daily or weekly tasks.
2. You must spend time on the activities that relate to your most important goals or you will not reach them.
3. You must fight the temptation to let urgent things keep you from doing important things.
4. You must master the mental and social game of time management so you can use your time productively, but without going crazy or losing your family and friends.

I discussed numbers 1 and 2 in this list in Chapter 3, in the context of planning. The next two sections cover numbers 3 and 4, while the rest of this chapter will give you systems and tools for practicing those tasks.

TIME MANAGEMENT MUSTS

- Have written goals and plans
- Spend time on tasks related to big goals
- Do what's important, not just what's urgent
- Master the mental and social aspects

Urgent Versus Important

If you wonder why you're working hard but making little progress toward your major goals, think about what you work on. Most of us work on the things that demand our immediate attention, or at least seem to demand it, rather than on the things that are really most important.

One major reason that the urgent supersedes the important is that we often feel that we're not in a position to control our time. And often we're not. Many organizations don't realize that people need time to (a) think and be creative, and (b) work on larger, longer-term, important projects and not just smaller, shorter-term, less important ones. As a result, people's responsibilities are set up in ways that keep them busy but not necessarily productive.

To keep the urgent and relatively unimportant in its place, and to manage your time in general, you have to:

Keep your major goals in mind: Keep your goals paramount among your priorities by writing about them in a journal, keeping a log of your progress, or hanging them on the wall (but move them now and then). That way, if something urgent arises and it relates to one of your major goals, you'll know it's important; if not, it's just urgent.

Learn to distinguish between the urgent and the important: You can, with practice, learn to quickly classify unexpected demands as well as scheduled tasks into one of four categories: the urgent and important; the urgent but unimportant; the important but not urgent; and the unimportant and not urgent. If you're spending time on non-urgent, unimportant tasks, you're not even trying to execute.

Identify the sources of urgency: What's creating the urgency that keeps you hopping? Is it customers with a problem? What's the problem? Can you find a broader solution? Is it your boss? What drives his or her demands? Keep a log for a week or so, or until you have enough data to discover the sources of all this urgency. We'll look at what to do about it later in this chapter.

Take a Look at Yourself

You might think of time as you would think of money. We develop time-usage habits in ways that are similar to the way we form spending habits. We plan major expenditures of time or money—for instance, time for major projects or money for major purchases—but we tend to spend smaller units of time and money almost unconsciously and out of habit.

Most of us learn some surprising things when we really track the ways in which we spend our money. All those vanilla lattes and take-out sushi meals add up to hundreds or even thousands of dollars per year.

Commuter Hell

I have had commutes ranging from ninety minutes to my current three minutes. I've commuted by car, train, subway, and foot. I realize you can think in the car, work on the train, observe your fellow man on the subway, and get exercise on foot. But the shorter your commute, the more control you have over your time. Long commutes generate real stress and expense. Think about it and consider your options.

You can experience similar surprises if you track your time.

Browsing the Web for laughs, talking aimlessly on the phone, reading articles long after you've got the point, and being a perfectionist about things that don't require it can easily chew up two hours or more each day. I'm not saying to totally omit these things—although they are good candidates for execution in the other sense of the term—but that you should know how much time you spend on them, and whether that time is well spent.

Then there are the major sinkholes, two of which are long commutes and long meetings. Anything you can do to limit the time you spend on either of these activities will more than repay itself. I understand that some people are stuck with long commutes and that some meetings are unavoidable, but as someone who has eliminated both from my life I can tell you that new vistas in productivity open up when you do away with them.

Modern Time Management

What I call classic time management is focused on defining tasks beforehand, tight scheduling, setting a brisk pace, and remembering that "Time is money." What I'm calling modern time management focuses more on the heart of the problem, which is not really a matter of scheduling or pacing but rather our thinking and behavior. This kind of time management got going with two books released in the 1970s: *The Time*

Trap by Alec MacKenzie and *How to Get Control of Your Time and Life* by Alan Lakein.

I recall Lakein's book being the more influential of the two, and I used his system to good effect for some years. Lakein also emphasized that our lives actually consist of time and that we have to relate our daily behaviors to our goals.

Basics of Lakein's System

Lakein's main contributions were to help readers identify or define major goals and then relate their daily and weekly activities and to-do lists to their goals. He recommended labeling each daily and weekly task an A, B, or C. The As were high priority because they would help you move toward important goals, or they had to get done because your boss or customers insisted. Bs had lower priority, and Cs the lowest.

The goal was to spend most of your time and energy on that day's As. If or when you finished that day's A or As, you would move on to the Bs, which really just amounts to a prioritized to-do list. People had been making to-do lists for decades, and many of those folks were prioritizing the items on the list. Lakein pushed readers to relate those As, Bs, and Cs to their goals, and not to fritter away time on Bs—let alone Cs—when there were As to be completed.

Lakein's Question

One of the best tips in *How to Get Control of Your Time and Life* is what the author calls Lakein's Question: "What is the best use of my time, right now?" Lakein allows that the best use of your time may well be sitting on your duff or sanding your nose on the beach. But during your work day, it's essential to avoid or quickly dispatch activities that do not represent the best use of your time at that time.

There are various ways to use Lakein's Question. You probably already ask it in some form from time to time. For instance, if you've ever said, "Why am I sitting in this meeting listening to this gasbag when I've got a major project due on Friday?" and then excused yourself from the meeting, then you've used Lakein's Question to good effect.

Lakein suggests using this question several times a day. Use it whenever you even suspect that you may be wasting your time, or even using it less than optimally.

My System

My system of time management involves choosing commitments carefully, timing myself often, and avoiding people and things that waste my time. By the latter, I mean people and things I dislike and those that I like but don't fit my schedule. Nothing earth-shattering there, but I have one more original technique, after I discuss these three general guidelines:

Choose Commitments Carefully

We've all had the experience of saying that we'll do something in the future and then, on the appointed

> Time is free, but it's priceless. You can't own it, but you can use it. You can't keep it, but you can spend it. Once you've lost it you can never get it back.
>
> —Harvey MacKay (entrepreneur and author)

day, realized that we don't want to, don't have time, or have something more important to do (like airing out our mailbox). If this happens to you often, analyze the patterns to find out why it's happening.

On the professional front: Are your coworkers, subordinates, or subcontractors pulling their weight? Are you doing only the things you do best, or are you trying to do everything? Is your company or boss wasting your time?

On the personal front: Are there people in your life who are overly demanding? Are you doing your children's homework for them? Are you over-committed to charitable organizations? Are you in the grip of habits that are neither productive nor enjoyable?

If so, you must eliminate or minimize your involvement in these situations. This may mean holding some heart-to-heart conversations with several people, perhaps including yourself. You must prepare for those conversations by considering your needs, the actual demands others are making on your time (it may be you, not them), and the outcome you want from the conversation.

Pulling back from a commitment, such as a charity or social obligation, can be done gradually or suddenly, explicitly or implicitly. However, there are right and wrong ways, and better and worse ways, of pulling back. Don't leave people flat, wondering if it was their breath that drove you away. Instead, in a clear but kind chat, tell them that you have to rear-range your schedule, that other demands have arisen, or that you just don't feel that you can give your best to the effort any more. If your boss is involved, talk in terms of productivity, priorities, and the good of the team.

Watching the Clock

I've noticed that I typically use whatever time I am given for a project. That's usually because I am juggling multiple projects, along with business devel-opment. But the work-expands-to-fill-the-time phe-nomenon is very real.

To force myself to work quickly, I will set a dead-line in hours or a specific time for completing a task, such as writing a chapter or assembling a mailing, and watch the clock to keep myself moving. The idea is to make a game of this, not to torture yourself. That way, the feedback on the time is motivating rather than anxiety-producing.

Avoiding Time Wasters

To avoid something, you must know it when you see it and then get out of its presence or get it out of yours. Study your behavior, preferable by keeping a time log for a few days. Be honest about what you log. Lying to yourself about how you spend your time is like lying to your doctor about your symptoms. Then elimi-nate, or at least minimize, time wasters—including the self-generated ones such as aimless Web brows-ing and pointless perfectionism.

Take Action
If you need help refusing requests, read *When I Say No, I Feel Guilty* by Manuel J. Smith (Bantam, 1985). Originally published in 1975, it's still one of the best books on the subject.

Many of us put up with time wasters in order to be polite or avoid hurt feelings. That's nice. But presumably these folks are not your loved ones or close friends, who should understand that you're working at the moment. So, if they're not loved ones or friends, who are they to impose on you? You don't owe them your time, only a bit of courtesy.

Dealing with "Talkers"

If you work as a salesperson, consultant, deal-maker, or entrepreneur you may find yourself enmeshed with people who like to talk, who are just fishing, or who just don't understand that you're working for a living. To deal with these folks I will typically:

TIMELY TIPS

- *You do not have to attend every event your significant other attends*

- *You are not obligated to answer the phone just because it rings*

- *You do not have to stop what you are doing for every interruption*

Ask for something in writing: Talking is a wonderful form of communication, but people have to put more thought into writing (except for stream-of-consciousness e-mails). I tell them to send me something and then I'll make up my mind. I'll also often direct them to my Web site or book for information.

High-Maintenance People

Do emotional vampires and one-way streeters really have a place in your life? If you find yourself giving but not getting in a relationship, ask yourself why. Some men and women feel they have to tolerate the intolerable in order to have a relationship, keep their job, or not "hurt" someone. Instead, talk to them about what you need and if you can't get it from them, dust.

Ask them to come to the point: Sometimes as they drone on I'll just say "faster" and they'll stop and say, "What?" and I'll say, "Can you move this along a bit faster? I don't need this much deep background."

Brush them off: Tell them that this sounds interesting, but you're not really the person they should be talking to. Repeat as necessary.

Charge them a fee: Tell them that you'd love to evaluate their idea, proposal, needs, deal, or whatever, but that you must charge them because you do this for a living. You can even charge for meetings at your hourly rate. This truly separates the serious from the non-serious.

> **NONE OF US** IS AS SMART AS ALL OF US.

—Ken Blanchard (author)

5 Parts of a Business and What They Do

At this point in history, the basic functions of a business—what a business needs to get done and the departments, people, and activities for getting them done—are well defined. You do not have to sit around wondering what a marketing and sales department does or what finance and accounting do. It's all been figured out.

However, business functions do not structure themselves, nor are they ever set in stone. For instance, information technology (IT) has revolutionized business over the past twenty years.

> **in•for•ma•tion tech•nol•o•gy (IT)**
>
> 1. computer, network, telephone, satellite, and other means of recording, storing, analyzing, and transmitting information
>
> 2. organizational function responsible for buying and maintaining IT equipment and services, also known as management information systems (MIS)

The personal computer and the Internet both increased and decreased the power of what had previously been called the data processing department. That function increased its power by integrating computers into every aspect of business, but decreased it by putting a networked computer on everyone's desk. People now "process" their data right there on their desks. So while the function's mission remained the same—to give people access to the information they need, and to prevent access by the wrong people—the ways in which the function does these things has changed.

In this chapter, we examine the key functions of a business and the main forms that a business can take in the United States—corporation, limited liability company, partnership, proprietorship. In one way or another most of these functions must be done by small businesses and nonprofit organizations, so we will touch on those as well.

Basic Theory of the Organization

The theory of the modern organization rests on three concepts, which people in the organization agree upon and are guided by in their organizational life:

- *Common purposes and goals*

- *Legitimate authority*

- *Division of labor*

Common Purposes and Goals

An organization is based on shared purposes and goals. Common purpose and goals ensure that everyone is "rowing in the same direction." If you do not agree with an organization's purpose and goals, if you do not believe that they are worth working toward, then you shouldn't be in the organization. Given the number and variety of organizations in this world, it should be possible to find one you can wholeheartedly support.

At times, an organization must change direction or even reinvent itself. It may have to find a new reason for being. In those instances, management will generally define the new purpose and goals, hopefully with input from the people in the organization. In those instances it is also common for some people to decide that they no longer want to be part of the organization and to move on. These are all natural and reasonable responses to change.

> Getting good players is easy. Getting them to play together is the hard part.
> —**Casey Stengel (coach, New York Yankees)**

Legitimate Authority

An organization must be run by people who can and will direct the energies and efforts of the people in the outfit. In business, these managers have authority based on the fact that they either are the owners or have been hired by and are paid by the owners. In most associations, managers are elected by the rank-and-file members or appointed by a board that was elected by the members. In democratic governments, where managers are usually referred to as administrators, officials, or bureaucrats (which is not always a negative term), they generally are either elected by the populace or hired or appointed by the elected officials.

To be truly legitimate, however, the authority of managers and leaders must also be based on competence and concern for the welfare of the organization and its stakeholders. If an owner decides to trash the business so he can use it as a tax write-off or a manager practices out-and-out nepotism, they will undercut managerial authority regardless of their legal or official status.

Division of Labor

Before the industrial revolution, most products were made by craftspeople, each of whom worked on a single unit. For instance, a cabinetmaker made a cabinet, and a shoemaker made a pair of shoes. However, even then people understood that some people are more skillful or productive at certain tasks than

nep•o•tism

1. hiring or promoting someone on the basis of family connections

2. practice that undermines the morale of non-family members of the organization

in•dus•tri•al rev•o•lu•tion

1. period in Britain in the late 1700s and early 1800s in which the economy developed rapidly due to the introduction of machines in the workplace

2. development in any nation where factories supplant agriculture and crafts

others. A sailmaker made the sails while carpenters worked on the hull. The proverbial butcher, baker, and candlestick maker represent division of labor.

An organization practices division of labor in that each function and person specializes in a task. Accountants keep the financial ledgers, salespeople find and win customers, and so on. None of the functions could stand on its own, and the whole is truly greater than the sum of its parts. The company can accomplish more than all of the people could if they were working individually.

Key Business Functions

In most sizable companies, the major functions or departments are:

- *Owners, board of directors, and senior management*

- *Finance*

- *Accounting*

- *Operations*

- *Marketing*

- *Sales*

- *Management Information Systems*

- *Support functions*

As I've noted and will discuss later in this chapter, most of these functions take place to some degree in most organizations whether large or small, profit or nonprofit.

Owners Run the Show

The owners, because the company is their property, either make the decisions regarding a company's goals, staffing, financing, resources, and activities, or delegate those decisions to management. In a proprietorship or a partnership the owners make those decisions directly.

It's a bit different in a corporation because owners own shares in the company rather than owning the company directly. If there are relatively few shareholders or if the shareholders are also the managers, then they direct the company as partners would. But if the corporation has many shareholders or if it is a publicly held company, then the owners elect a board of directors to act in their place. The board of directors hires the senior managers, typically the chief executive officer (CEO) and the chief operating officer (COO), who in turn hire the rest of the management team, which hires the staff.

pub•lic•ly held com•pa•ny

1. corporation that sells ownership shares, in the form of stock, to the public

2. company subject to regulation by the Securities Exchange Commission

Finance Controls the Cash

Finance controls the money flowing into, out of, and through a company. I'll discuss financial management in Chapter 6, but it is basically the responsibility of the finance function. To distinguish it from accounting, you might think of finance as dealing with the decision-making aspects of the organization's money while accounting deals with the record-keeping aspects. Of course, accounting makes decisions and recommendations as well, but it is finance—along with the CEO and COO—that makes the major decisions about how to raise and invest the organization's money.

Finance works with the senior executives to set revenue and profit goals for the year and helps the other functions prepare their budgets and consolidates them into one overall budget for the company. An organization's financial managers work with banks and other lenders and investors to ensure that the company has access to funds. The company uses these funds to purchase or lease equipment and real estate, and otherwise finance the organization's growth.

> **budg•et**
>
> 1. planned and estimated levels of sales, expenses, and other sources and uses of funds for a specific period, such as a month, quarter, or year
>
> 2. key tools for making financial plans and decisions and controlling money

Funding Growth

Companies fund growth through internal sources, mainly profits and the owners' money, and external sources, such as loans, which have to be repaid, and funds from investors, who share in the profits instead of being paid back. Companies use external sources when they cannot finance their growth completely through internal sources—for instance when the company is new, faces huge opportunities, or isn't generating enough cash.

Accounting Does the Counting

Accounting monitors and records the flow of money into and out of the organization. While a small business many have a single accountant or bookkeeper—or the owner—taking care of all aspects of this, larger ones delegate the tasks to the following areas:

- *Accounts receivable bills customers and clients for the products and services the company sells and makes sure the bills get paid.*

- *Accounts payable tracks expenditures and authorizes payments to suppliers, lenders, and so on.*

- *Payroll makes sure that employees get paid.*

- *Credit and collections decides how much credit (or trade credit) the company extends to a customer. If you get bills from MasterCard or Visa, you're familiar with credit. If you get calls from them when those bills are past due, then you're also familiar with collections.*

Business customers with good payment records can buy hundreds of thousands of dollars worth of goods on credit, meaning they are given an extended amount of time in which to pay the bill. This is done in most businesses that sell expensive or high-volume goods or services because credit makes it easy for customers to buy, and thus easier for the company to make sales.

Accounting is staffed mainly by, you guessed it, accountants. These professionals are trained in accounting practices and regulations and in tax laws and procedures. Usually they work in a specific area, such as accounts receivable or accounts payable, and move among these functions. Certain staff accountants also work with the external accounting firms, if the organization uses them.

Operations: Core of the Company

In general, operations produces and delivers the product or service that the organization is set up to sell to customers. In most manufacturing companies, operations centers on the factory in which the company makes its products. I say "most" because some companies that appear to be manufacturers actually hire contract manufacturers. These are production facilities that make products to another company's specifications to be marketed and distributed by that company.

Operations also includes shipping and receiving, where the company ships products to its customers and receives materials from its suppliers. The purchasing department, which buys materials and supplies, and the warehouse and transportation facilities are also part of operations. In a manufacturing company, the core of operations is the production function, which is called operations or just production.

In a service organization (one that sells services, such as a bank or a brokerage firm), operations includes the employees who serve the customers and the places where they work. For example, in a bank operations would include the branch locations. Operations also includes "back-office" functions in a service organization, activities that customers don't see but that have to do with processing customer transactions. Check-processing in a bank is a back-office function.

Managers in operations are responsible for employee productivity, cost control, and quality. In most companies, people in operations do what most of us think of as the actual work of the company. In a manufacturing outfit, they are the production workers and their managers. In a service firm, they usually work directly with customers or just behind the scenes to deliver the service.

Marketing Sells to Groups

It's useful to think of marketing as the process of selling a product or service to groups of people or businesses, as opposed to sales, which is done one-on-one. Marketing gets the story of the company's products and services out to potential customers through advertising, promotions, direct mail, special events, and other means. These efforts prompt customers to place their orders, invite them to inquire about the company's products or services, make them more receptive to the company's salespeople, or some combination of these responses.

The marketing function can include market research, which studies customers and prospects to learn about their characteristics, needs, motivations, and buying behavior; product development, which devises new ways to meet customers' needs; and public relations, which works to have the company covered by, or at least mentioned in, the media.

Prompt a Response

The best marketing efforts, particularly for small outfits, seek a response. The results of advertising just to increase awareness are harder to measure, so if possible ask for action when you advertise. An ad or letter can prompt readers to call a toll-free number, feature a coupon or a limited-time offer, or encourage people to visit a Web site or another way to get more information. Any response you can measure helps you gauge marketing's effectiveness.

Sales Brings in the Money

The sales function sells the company's products or services by presenting them to customers and potential customers on the telephone, in person, or both. In some companies salespeople sell to distributors or retailers who resell the product. They may sell to individuals or to businesses, to one-time buyers or to major accounts. It's a critical part of the business. Salespeople persuade customers to pull out their wallets and checkbooks and pay for a product or service, which isn't easy.

Take Action
To learn more about actual selling, see the book on *Persuasion* in this Adams Media series.

In many companies, the sales function includes customer service, which works to make sure customers are satisfied with their purchase and to resolve any problems that arise after the sale.

MIS Means Information

As noted at the start of this chapter, management information systems (MIS) runs the company's digital information systems. This department has become extremely important because information itself is now recognized as a strategic resource. Formerly known as data processing in most companies, it is now key in most businesses, especially large service businesses. MIS oversees and executes the purchasing, programming, maintenance, and security of the company's computers. This department defines company requirements for computers, software, and related items and purchases, installs, programs, and maintains them.

MIS is mainly staffed by computer systems analysts and software programmers. Systems analysts work to define and meet the company's hardware needs, while programmers work on the software needs.

Organizational Supporters

Functions other than those I've covered in this chapter are support functions. Technically you could call accounting, finance, and MIS support functions, because they are not marketing and sales (which interface with customers) or operations (which makes the products or delivers the services that the company sells). However, here I am including the following support functions:

Human resources: The human resources department (or "HR") works with the managers of other departments to attract, hire, retain, and train employees and to ensure that the company is in compliance with government employment regulations. Human resources also ensures that employee benefit programs are in place.

Legal department: Staffed mostly by attorneys and their assistants, the legal department (or "legal") ensures that the company complies with laws and regulations and handles lawsuits, whether they are brought by the company or against the company.

Investor relations: The marketing department in a publicly held company will usually include an investor relations function, or it may be a freestanding area apart from marketing. Investor relations communicates with the company's shareholders and potential investors, and organizes the annual meeting of shareholders.

Facilities management: Facilities management (or "facilities") oversees the maintenance and upkeep of the company's building and the heating and cooling system. Related functions might include telecommunications and security.

Support functions basically support all of the other departments that are making something, selling something, or dealing with money.

What About Small Companies?

You will find the aforementioned functions in most large companies. A small business may not have specific departments devoted to each activity, but many of those activities will still be performed in small companies. For instance, every business has to prepare budgets, keep financial records, pay taxes, and finance growth. Every business has to market and sell a product or service. Every outfit, except for one- or two-person shops, has to attract and hire good employees and obey the employment laws, which typically apply

Independents to the Rescue

One side effect of the trend toward smaller staffs and outsourcing is the number of highly skilled independent contractors. While many of them want full-time employers, many don't. Therefore, you can find not only writers, graphic designers, and other traditional freelancers, but also marketing, HR, and financial managers, and even chief executive officers, for temporary or part-time hire.

only to companies that hire true employees or, in some states, a certain number of employees.

Small or new companies may be able to do without some, or even most, of these departments. However, as a company grows, once the activities become frequent enough and complex enough to require specialists, a specialist should be appointed or hired and the function should be formalized.

At the most basic level, a small professional services firm such as a law practice, consulting firm, or ad agency, will have an office manager or a business manager to deal with the administrative aspects of the business and, probably, a bookkeeper (who represents the accounting function). Such a company would also probably have one partner or "rainmaker" who brings in most of the business; that person amounts to the sales department. A consulting firm or ad agency might have someone designated as the project manager and who more or less amounts to the operations manager. It might also have an outside marketing communications or public relations person. This independent contractor prepares sales letters, and perhaps a monthly newsletter, runs the Web site, and embodies the marketing function. Finance, or rather financial decisions, would be handled by the owner or owners, who are also the senior managers.

So, most of the basic functions of an organization must be executed no matter how large or small the outfit. It's really a matter of who does it, and how formal and well funded the effort should be. Common mistakes entrepreneurs make include trying to do everything themselves, giving responsibility for functions to people who lack the needed skills, and failing to see that they need a more formal function when they do. When the company needs a person to carry out a specific activity or function, then it should hire that person, if only as a freelancer or a part-timer at the start.

Four Types of Businesses

A business can be organized in one of four basic ways—as a proprietorship, partnership, corporation, or limited liability company.

A proprietorship is owned by an individual. That person, the proprietor, owns the business and the profits it generates and is personally responsible for its debts.

A partnership is a business owned by two or more individuals who formally agree to contribute their funds and other resources to the business and to share its profits. A limited partner (sometimes called a "silent partner") contributes funding, but does not make management decisions or participate actively in the business. A general partner contributes money, makes management decisions, and participates actively in the business. Many consulting firms and professional services firms are organized as partnerships. General partners are personally liable for the financial obligations of the business. The liability of limited partners is limited to the amount of their investment, which is why they're called limited partners. Also, a decision or act by a general partner binds all of the partners to that decision or act.

A corporation is a legal structure in which the owners are not personally liable for the financial obligations of the business. They can lose only the money they invest in the corporation. That investment occurs when they contribute money to fund the start-up of the business or, later, when they buy stock in the company. A corporation is often referred to as a "legal person," because it can own property, enter into contracts, initiate lawsuits, and be sued.

The three main advantages of a corporation for the owners are:

- *Limited liability for the company's debts or actions, for instance lawsuits against the company*

- *Ability to raise money in the stock and bond markets*

- *Ownership that can be easily sold or transferred by selling the stock*

A limited liability company (not limited liability corporation) is a relatively new form of business organization that has become popular. A limited liability company, or LLC, provides some benefits of both partnerships and corporations. As in a partnership, the earnings flow through to the owners, who are taxed at their personal tax rates. This does away with the "double taxation" that occurs when a corporation pays its income tax and then the owners pay personal income taxes when the earnings are distributed to them as dividends. Owners of an LLC also have the limited liability that owners of a corporation enjoy. LLC owners are not personally responsible for the debts of the company, nor are they liable for debts arising from lawsuits. Also, an LLC is easy to administer because in most states there are no requirements to hold quarterly meetings of the owners and to keep minutes of the meetings, as there are for corporations.

MANAGING MONEY, PROJECTS, AND PROCESSES

part 2

> **WATCH THE PENNIES**
> AND THE DOLLARS WILL TAKE CARE
> OF THEMSELVES.

—Benjamin Franklin
(author and publisher)

6

Managing Money: Income, Outgo, Profit, and Loss

Next to time, money is the most important resource to be managed in any execution effort, and it is equally easy to mismanage. Managing money calls for information, planning, and discipline. This chapter covers the basics of financial management, ways and means of tracking income and outgo, and financial decisions. (We'll look at the decisions themselves in Chapter 7.)

Biggest Money Mistakes

Leaving aside the psychological issues that prevent people from seeking prosperity (which I cover in the book, *Motivation*, in this Adams Media series), people and organizations tend to make five basic mistakes when it comes to money:

re•turn

1. amount of money earned on an investment in an asset, activity, or company

2. often expressed as a percentage of the amount invested

3. non-monetary benefit of an activity, such as exercise or intellectual pursuits

Ignoring information about money: To manage money you need information on your income and outgo, and on the returns generated on money put into various activities and assets.

Failing to control spending: As you know, it is far easier to spend money than it is to make it. Worse, money spent or invested may fail to generate an acceptable return for the amount of the outlay, and you could even fail to recoup your invested capital. For these reasons, an entity must constantly evaluate and re-evaluate spending decisions.

Taking on too much debt: Given that it's easier to spend money than to make it, many people and organizations borrow to finance spending. Not all debt is bad. For instance, it makes sense to take on debt to finance a productive activity (such as sales effort) or an asset (such as a computer) that will increase your revenue or income. But borrowing to finance nonproductive activities does not make sense.

Failing to grow income: Expenses tend to increase over time because there's always a bit of inflation in the economy and it's human nature to want more. So a household or organization should generally aim to grow its income or revenue.

Fixating too much on money: This mistake may seem out of place here, but fixating too much on growing revenue or reducing costs can blind people to larger realities. For a person, this might mean health and family concerns. For a company, this might mean market conditions or core mission. Money is one aspect of execution—not the entirety.

> ## in · fla · tion
>
> 1. increase in prices caused when demand exceeds supply
>
> 2. erosion of the spending power of money when prices rise faster than incomes

Start with Information

As I mentioned in Chapter 5, information about money has become as important as money. In a way, that's always been true. Information about money comes in many forms, ranging from checkbook stubs and restaurant receipts to budgets and variance reports, financial statements, and, of course, income tax forms.

In the rest of this chapter I'll cover basic budgeting concepts, and then the two key types of financial statements. If you already know this material, this will be a review. If you don't, I suggest

Take Action
Nonprofits face most of the same financial management challenges that businesses face. Visit *www.managementhelp .org/finance/np_fnce/ np_fnce.htm* for an excellent guide to financial management for nonprofit organizations.

that you focus on the concepts rather than the technical terms. The technical terms are fairly straightforward, but the concepts are the important thing.

Budgets and Variances

The budget is the key tool in any situation involving money. A budget is a plan that allocates amounts to specific elements of income and outgo over a certain period. For instance, a sales budget shows the amount of revenue a company expects to bring in during a period. A travel budget allocates money to expenses such as airfare, lodging, and meals.

I hope you're already familiar with budgeting, but many of us are not. Instead of budgeting, many people, including some business people, simply watch money come and go without attempting to control it. The budget is the basic tool for controlling money.

Here is a sample annual budget for a one-person consulting business. Column 1 shows the budgeted amounts, which the owner/consultant estimated and planned at the beginning of the year. Column 2 shows the actual amounts that came in and went out. Column 3 shows the variances between the actual and budgeted amounts. Amounts in parentheses are lower than the budgeted amount, or are negative.

Here are a few points about this budget and variance report:

Sample Budget and Variance Report

	BUDGET	ACTUAL	VARIANCE
Income:			
Sales (consulting fees)	$160,000	$150,000	($10,000)
Investments	$5,000	$3,000	($2,000)
Other (speaking fees, etc.)	$5,000	$7,000	$2,000
Total Income	$170,000	$160,000	($10,000)
Expenses:			
Office Rent	$9,000	$9,000	0
Telephone	$3,000	$2,000	($1,000)
Web Site and Internet	$1,000	$1,500	$500
Direct Mail and Advertising	$2,000	$1,000	($1,000)
Disability and Health Insurance	$16,000	$18,000	$2,000
Travel, Meals, and Lodging	$3,000	$4,000	$1,000
Client Meals and Entertainment	$2,000	$2,500	$500
Professional Fees	$8,000	$9,500	$1,500
Publications	$1,000	$500	($500)
Total Expenses	$45,000	$48,000	$3,000
Pre-Tax Income (total income- total expenses)	$125,000	$112,000	
Surplus (Shortfall)			($13,000)

- I didn't budget for new savings or new debt, which a business or household normally would. This was to underscore the concept of the surplus or shortfall in cash. A surplus can be saved, invested, or used to pay off debt. A shortfall must be financed somehow. That means taking on new debt, which you typically want to avoid.

- For simplicity, I left out federal and state income taxes.

- As you can see, the consultant booked $10,000 less in fees than he had anticipated, and earned $2,000 less on investments and $2,000 more in other income than budgeted.

- The consultant didn't do a bad job of controlling expenses—just not a particularly good one. He should have reduced expenses further, given the lower-than-expected fee income. This can be hard to do if the cost of certain necessities rises, as was the case with health insurance here, or if you must spend money to make money, as was the case with the travel, meals, and entertainment.

General Budgeting Guidelines

This report and process would be similar for a project or for a department in a company. In general,

Budget Mindfully

View each new budget period with fresh eyes. Where can you find more business or other income? Where can you cut costs without hurting the business? That's where the creativity is in budgeting. In fact, in zero-based budgeting you budget from scratch, as if the business were just starting. What would you include and exclude, and what would you do differently, if you were just starting up? It can be a useful approach.

budgeting calls for projecting your sources of income and allocating that income, and other available funds, to your expenses. (Areas of the business that do not bring in money, such as the IT department, have only expense budgets.)

One way to allocate expenses is to examine the budgets and variances from the previous period and plan accordingly. Yet you must know the reasons for variances. Why did you spend more or less than you budgeted last year on a given item? Was it a one-shot event or a permanent trend? Do not mindlessly use the previous year's numbers for the next year's budget.

Budgetary Control

A budget is useless unless you track your expenses and make the adjustments needed to stay on budget or to reduce expenses. Also be sure to plan to finance any shortfall that could occur. This may mean having a line of credit in place or taking a loan, but that should be temporary. If you run a shortfall year after year, you must change the way you do business so you either make more money or spend less. There really is no other solution.

Basic Financial Statements

Aside from budgets and variance reports, financial statements—and the accounts that make them up—are the main tools that organizations use to understand their financial status and performance.

I'm going to cover the balance sheet and the income statement here. The cash flow statement is also important, but it is derived from the accounts found in these statements. My aim is to convey the basic financial concepts, and those reside on the balance sheet and income statement.

Balance Sheet: A Financial Snapshot

The balance sheet is often called a snapshot of the business. It is compiled from the asset and liability accounts on a specific date, usually the end of a fiscal year or quarter.

Essentially, the balance sheet lists the company's accounts and their value on a specific date. The key accounts and presentation in the balance sheet are as follows:

Financial statements are shown for at least two periods, usually the most recent year and the previous year. That allows you to compare the accounts

ABC Company: Balance Sheet

	12/31/07	12/31/06
ASSETS		
Current Assets:		
Cash and Marketable Securities	$2,600,000	$1,520,000
Accounts Receivable	$4,000,000	$3,800,000
Inventories	$5,400,000	$6,000,000
Total Current Assets	$12,000,000	$11,320,000
Property, Plant, and Equipment		
Buildings and Machinery	$10,600,000	$9,990,000
Less: Accumulated Depreciation	$3,600,000	$3,000,000
Total Property, Plant and Equipment	$7,000,000	$6,990,000
Other Assets		
Intangibles (goodwill, patents)	$400,000	$380,000
Total Assets	**$19,400,000**	**$18,690,000**
LIABILITIES AND OWNERS' EQUITY		
Current Liabilities		
Accounts Payable	$2,000,000	$1,880,000
Short-Term Loans	$1,700,000	$1,800,000
Accrued Expenses	$660,000	$600,000
Income Taxes Payable	$640,000	$380,000
Current Portion of Long-Term Debt	$400,000	$400,000
Total Current Liabilities	$5,400,000	$5,060,000
Long-Term Liabilities		
Long-Term Debt	$5,000,000	$5,400,000
Total Liabilities	$10,400,000	$10,460,000
Owners' Equity		
Common Stock	$3,000,000	$3,000,000
Additional Paid-In Capital	$1,400,000	$1,400,000
Retained Earnings	$4,600,000	$3,830,000
Total Owners' Equity	$9,000,000	$8,230,000
Total Liabilities and Owners' Equity	**$19,400,000**	**$18,690,000**

from period to period. These accounts are maintained by the accounting staff or bookkeeper, who records transactions in the relevant accounts. At the end of the period, the accounts are summed to construct the balance sheet.

Here is a brief explanation of each account:

Assets Explained

Cash and Marketable Securities: Cash is money in the company's checking and savings accounts, and petty cash in the office. Marketable securities are safe, short-term investments, often U.S. government securities.

Accounts Receivable: Money owed to the company by customers who have purchased goods or services on credit. Unfortunately, some customers don't pay their bills, so there is usually an allowance for bad debt on the balance sheet. I've omitted this for simplicity.

Inventories: Finished products for sale to customers or products in the manufacturing process. Service companies typically do not sell products, and thus usually carry no inventory.

Property, Plant, and Equipment: Buildings, such as offices, factories, and warehouses; equipment, such as machinery, computers, and furniture; and fixtures, like display cases. These assets depreciate over time, and the accumulated depreciation is a running total of the depreciation charged to that asset over time, so the balance sheet reflects the true worth of the assets.

Intangibles: Assets such as trademarks and patents that have value even though they do not physically exist.

> ## de•pre•ci•a•tion
>
> 1. value of an asset that is charged against that asset during a period
>
> 2. allocating the cost of an asset over its life, rather than in one year

Liabilities and Owners' Equity Explained

Accounts Payable: Amounts the company owes to its suppliers. (Note that one company's receivable is another's payable.)

Short-Term Loans Payable: Borrowings from a bank or another party for less than one year.

Accrued Expenses: Money owed (other than loans) to companies and individuals, including employees, and to vendors who have not yet been paid.

Income Taxes Payable: This account is just what it sounds like. These are income taxes that have been accrued but are not yet due.

Current Portion of Long-Term Debt: This is the amount of a long-term loan that is due to be paid within one year of the balance sheet date.

Long-Term Debt: All debt due after one year from the date of the balance sheet.

Owner's Equity: The financial stake the owners have in the company. After you subtract liabilities from assets you have the total amount of owner's equity, which typically takes three forms.

Stock: Stock represents ownership shares in a corporation. That is, the stockholders own the company. Companies sell stock to raise money from investors, and investors buy stock in order to share in the company's profits in the form of dividends.

Additional Paid-In Capital: When a company issues stock, the stock has a par value, a value assigned by the company (for example, $1, $5, or $12 a share). This does not determine the stock's selling price—that is determined in the market. The amount paid to the company in excess of the par value of the stock is counted as additional paid-in capital. It is capital paid into the company in addition to the stock's par value.

Retained Earnings: A company can either distribute earnings to the owners or reinvest them in the business to finance growth. Retained earnings accumulate over time and become part of the capital that finances the company.

ABC Corp. Income Statement

	2007	2006
SALES	$22,000,000	$20,400,000
Cost of Goods Sold	$16,400,000	$15,400,000
GROSS INCOME	$5,600,000	$5,000,000
Selling, General, and Admin.		
Expenses	$2,800,000	$2,650,000
Depreciation Expense	$600,000	$550,000
OPERATING INCOME	$2,200,000	$1,800,000
Other Expenses:		
Interest Expense	$270,000	$300,000
Other Income		
Interest on Marketable		
Securities	$100,000	$80,000
INCOME BEFORE TAXES	$2,030,000	$1,580,000
Provision for Income Taxes	$960,000	$730,000
NET INCOME (LOSS)	$1,070,000	$850,000

Income Statement: Performance in a Period

In contrast to the balance sheet, the income statement records the business's financial performance in a period. It is a record of the money earned and spent in the period, and it shows whether or not the company made money; thus it is also called the profit and loss statement, or P&L.

The income statement starts with the total sales figure, subtracts expenses, and adds other, non-sales income such as interest income, to arrive at net income—the bottom line.

The key distinction in expenses is between cost of goods sold and other expenses. Cost of goods sold relates mainly to manufacturers. It's the costs of materials and labor used to produce the goods sold in the period. The other major cost is selling, general, and administrative expenses (or SG&A), which includes most other expenses.

The Income Statement Accounts

Sales: This top line totals the company's sales in the period.

Cost of Goods Sold: This is just want it sounds like, the amount it cost the company to produce the goods, mainly materials and labor costs.

Gross Income: Sales minus the cost of goods sold equals gross income. When expressed as a percentage of sales, this is a gross margin. Separating income like this lets managers manage the cost of producing products separately from the cost of selling them and running the rest of the business.

Selling, General, and Administrative Expense: SG&A includes the cost of selling the products or services, management salaries, and other expenses of running the company.

Depreciation Expense: This is the amount of depreciation charged against the value of assets during the period. Calculations for depreciation are a bit technical and beyond the scope of this book.

Operating Income: This is the amount earned from the actual operations of the business—by making and selling the company's goods and services—as opposed to money earned in interest or by selling off assets.

Other Expenses and Other Income: This account totals up expenses and income not related to operations, such as interest expense and interest income, as shown here. It would also include expenses for, or money awarded in, lawsuits.

Income before Taxes and Net Income: These are just what they say. The provision for income taxes accounts for the taxes owed for the period. If a company has a loss, it usually does not owe any taxes.

Fixed Costs and Variable Costs

Most businesses have a mix of fixed costs and variable costs. Fixed costs remain the same regardless of the production or sales volume. For example, the rent or mortgage on the building, insurance, and managers' salaries are fixed costs. Some, but not all, fixed costs are considered overhead—costs not directly associated with production or sales.

Take Action
For an excellent glossary of accounting terms, visit *www.accountz.com/glossary.html*.

Variable costs change with the volume of products and services the company produces and sells. These include wages for production and sales staff, materials, and telephone, travel, and lodging for salespeople. Layoffs are common because labor is the largest variable cost for most companies.

Sound financial management generally calls for keeping fixed costs low, especially in a new or small business. If sales decrease because of a recession or new competition, you can cut your variable costs and try to sell harder. But if you're stuck with high fixed costs, your business can get killed when sales decrease.

Financial Statements and Execution

Let's get back to execution. What have these statements got to do with it? Well, however you go about it and whatever you call them, you are going to be dealing with financial concepts and the concrete realities they represent.

Superb execution calls for marshaling and directing the factors of production toward the most useful activities given the goals you are trying to achieve and your plan for achieving them. Virtually all of those factors of production and the activities they're employed in are represented, or can be represented, in budgets, variance reports, accounts, and financial statements.

Take Action

Get a copy of *Finance for the Non-Financial Manager* by Gene Siciliano (McGraw-Hill, 2003) for a more detailed introduction to general financial management.

For instance, if you have an asset that's not making money or not making enough money, there's a good chance that you should sell it—or even give it away—and use the resulting money or space for a more productive asset. Indeed, every asset should be dedicated to the activity that will enable it to earn the highest return, and if there are no activities that would employ the asset and earn an acceptable return, the asset should probably be sold.

I'll discuss basic financial management in Chapter 10, which is about managing growth.

> **WHENEVER YOU SEE A SUCCESSFUL BUSINESS, SOMEONE ONCE MADE A COURAGEOUS DECISION.**
>
> —Peter Drucker (author and management consultant)

7

Making Sound Decisions

You might think that, with the collective experience we have in various endeavors, and the practices developed over more than 100 years of management history, decision making would be a fairly easy matter. Sometimes it is. Routine decisions can be made according to policies and procedures.

But that's not the kind of decision we're concerned with in this chapter. Here, we focus on the larger decisions involved in formulating and executing a plan. These decisions involve significant commitments of money, people, time, and resources, typically without clear policies or procedures to guide you.

There are, however, tools, and we'll be looking at some of those that enable managers and entrepreneurs to make decisions. These standard methods developed as the management profession became more professionalized, and they offer time-tested methods for gathering, organizing, analyzing, and evaluating the information you need to make sound decisions.

Six Steps to Decent Decisions

It usually helps to have a framework or process for important activities. There's really no recipe for good decisions, but you can improve your chances by following this six-step process.

> When you have to make a choice and you don't make it, that itself is a choice.
> —**William James** (author)

1. Define the problem. Most decisions either relate to a problem or can be framed as a problem, so you must define the problem properly. Don't confuse the symptom of the problem with the cause of the problem. For instance, if your organization is experiencing high employee turnover, that's the symptom. The cause could be low pay, incompetent management, poor opportunities for advancement, stultifying job content, or incorrect employee expectations. Each of these calls for a different solution.

2. Gather information. Good decisions require good information. Once you define the problem, gather all the relevant facts and figures—or at least as many as you can gather with a reasonable expenditure of time and money. Regardless of the method used to gather them, you have to have facts and figures in hand or you are guessing rather than deciding.

3. Analyze the information. Facts and figures themselves rarely provide the whole story, and when they don't you may need analytical tools to help you understand them. We'll examine a few of these tools in this chapter.

4. Develop options. When you face a decision, you need to have choices. You may not like any of the choices, but even among odious options usually one is less unpleasant than the others. Generally, however, if you understand the cause of the problem, you can develop one or more reasonably attractive alternatives. Sometimes you may have only one option, and the decision is to execute that course of action or not, but these situations should be rare if you openly consider all potential solutions.

5. Choose and implement the best option. If you followed the first four steps, you will probably make a good decision—or at least a defensible one. Take care, however, to avoid "analysis paralysis."

6. Monitor the outcome. It's rarely possible just to make a decision and forget about it. You usually have to monitor the outcome to learn how the decision worked and make any necessary adjustments. This may entail improving

---

a·nal·y·sis pa·raly·sis

1. putting off a decision indefinitely in order to gather and consider more information

2. often results when people are perfectionists or dread making mistakes

or correcting mistakes in execution, trying another option, or even reexamining the problem.

A decision-making process need not be a big deal. For example, for small decisions, fact-finding may mean one or two phone calls. Your list of options may be to do it or don't do it. But even in small decisions, this process will help you. Meanwhile, major decisions always require information, analysis, and clear thinking about options.

Take Action
For a clear look at economic rationales in decision making, see *Making Great Decisions in Business and Life* by David R. Henderson and Charles L. Hooper (Chicago Park Press, 2005).

An actual decision-making process promotes rational business decisions that can be explained to others. Even if your decision doesn't work out, you'll at least be able to answer the question, "What were you thinking?"

Decisions about Resources

Many business decisions involve allocating resources, such as money, labor, materials, and equipment. Even the largest businesses operate with limited resources, so managers must decide what allocation of resources will be the best, which usually means the most profitable.

For instance, here are typical resource allocation decisions that managers face:

> o *How much should we invest in developing a new product or acquiring a business?*

- What's the best size for our business? How much staff and space do we need?

- Which piece of equipment should we buy, the more expensive or the less expensive?

- When should we open and close for business?

- Which of two or more possible locations for a business is better?

Managers need tools that will help them make these decisions. Five tools and guidelines that most managers use in such decisions are:

- Cost-benefit analysis

- Crossover analysis

- Law of diminishing returns

- Economies of scale

- Decision trees

Cost-Benefit Analysis

There are various tools for conducting cost-benefit

> ### cost-ben•e•fit a•nal•y•sis
>
> 1. method for assessing and comparing the expected costs and benefits of a decision
>
> 2. way of considering dollar costs rather than emotional or social costs

analyses, and we'll look at two of them—benefit analysis and crossover analysis—in the next two sections.

For now, let's consider the general notion of cost-benefit analysis by looking at a pizza parlor in a major city. Like any store owner, the pizza man has to decide when to open and when to close. In making this decision, he might check the hours of other eateries in the area, and maybe ask some customers who come in early or late how they'd respond to his opening later or closing earlier. But the key factor is the cost versus the benefit of opening earlier or closing later.

Let's say that the pizza man found out long ago that he has to open at 11 A.M., when customers start arriving. But he's been closing at midnight more or less out of habit and he's not sure that's worth it.

After reviewing his sales and expense figures for the past six months, he has the data he needs for a cost-benefit analysis. He knows the cost of staying open that last hour, and he knows the average amount of money he makes in that last hour. Indeed, he has calculated that it costs him $22 to stay open from 11 P.M. to midnight. This includes the cost of electricity for the lights, gas for the oven, heat in the winter, and pay for his assistant who cleans up and helps him close. If the pizza man closes at 11 P.M., he saves that $22.

On the benefit side, he must calculate the profit on the pies he sells in that last hour. His accountant recently calculated that between whole pies and slices he makes an average profit of $9.00 a pie. The sales figures show that he sells an average of three pies in that last hour. Thus, he makes an average of $27.00 (three pies times $9.00 a pie) in that last hour of operation. That's the benefit.

In cost-benefit analysis the key question is: "Does the benefit outweigh the cost?"

It does in this case. If you take the benefit of $27 and subtract the cost of $22, you get $5. This is also known as the net benefit. On a pure cost-benefit basis, it is worth it for the pizza man to stay open that last hour.

However, other factors may be worth considering. For instance, if the assistant wants to start going home earlier or if late-night crime is rising, the owner may decide it's just not worth it to stay open the extra hour for $5, even though on a pure cost-benefit basis, it is worth it.

Of course this is just an illustration. You can imagine how complex the analysis becomes when an automobile manufacturer analyzes the decision to develop a new model or build a new factory. The key point is that a manager looks at most situations in terms of costs and benefits.

Let's turn to another way of analyzing costs and benefits: crossover analysis.

net ben•e•fit

1. benefit in dollars minus the cost in dollars

2. when positive, indicates a decision is justified on a pure cost-benefit basis

cross•o•ver a•nal•y•sis

1. method for calculating the unit volume when the cost of two machines with different costs is equal

2. unit volume where you should switch from one product or service to another

Crossover Analysis

As a manager or entrepreneur, you will sometimes have to choose to buy one of two or more similar pieces of equipment. Usually, each will have its own set of fixed and variable costs (which I explained in Chapter 6—in this case, fixed being the cost of the machine itself and variable being paper and toner). How do you decide which machine to buy?

Suppose you are a copy shop owner and you can buy one of two copiers. Machine One has fixed costs of $10,000 and variable costs of 2 cents a copy. Machine Two has fixed costs of $5,000 and variable costs of 4 cents a copy.

To put these numbers and the two options on a comparable footing, you need to calculate the crossover point. This is the unit volume at which the cost of the two machines is equal. Then you can make the decision based on the volume of copies you expect to make.

Here's the formula:

Crossover units =
(Machine Two's fixed costs − Machine One's fixed costs)
(Machine One's variable costs − Machine Two's variable costs)

Crossover units = $\frac{(5,000 - 10,000)}{(.02 - .04)}$

Crossover units = $\frac{(-\$5,000)}{(-.02)}$

Crossover units = 250,000 copies

The total cost of the two machines, that is fixed and variable costs together, is equal at 250,000 copies per year. Above and below that volume, one machine is preferable to the other. To see which one is preferable on which side of the crossover volume, you calculate the cost of each machine at a unit volume just below the crossover point and just above that point.

For instance, at 240,000 copies the cost of each machine is as follows:

Machine One $(240,000 \times \$0.02) + \$10,000 = \$14,800$
Machine Two $(240,000 \times \$0.04) + \$5,000 = \$14,600$

These two calculations tell us that Machine Two is the cheaper one at 240,000 copies.

At 260,000 units the cost of each machine is as follows:

Machine One $(260,000 \times \$0.02) + \$10,000 = \$15,200$
Machine Two $(260,000 \times \$0.04) + \$5,000 = \$15,400$

These two calculations tell us that Machine One is the cheaper one at 260,000 copies.

So we see that Machine Two, the one with the lower fixed costs, will be preferable below the crossover point, and Machine One will be preferable above that point.

Business people have developed many tools for analyzing financial and production information, so they can make rational decisions. We cover only a few in this chapter.

Splendid Spreadsheets

Crossover calculations are a good example of the analysis that you can easily do in a spreadsheet program such as Microsoft Excel. You define the elements and operations of the formulas in the cells, plug in the values, do the calculation, and get your answer. You can then easily change one or more values while holding the others constant and see the effect of increases and decreases in any value.

Enough Already! The Law of Diminishing Returns

It's one of the oldest questions in the world: "How much is enough?" The law of diminishing returns helps you answer that, especially with regard to resources (except money). The law of diminishing returns is based on the notion that you get some return—more speed, quality, efficiency, or effectiveness—with each unit of a resource you add to a business or project, but then, at some point you get a lower return.

The classic example is workers in a field. They may be planting or harvesting, but whatever they're doing they will be able to do it better with more workers—until they start bumping into one another, whacking each other with their farm implements, or stomping all over the planted rows or the harvested crops. The point of diminishing returns is the point at which that one additional worker adds less efficiency than the one who was added before.

Figure 7-1 depicts this graphically. The vertical axis is the number of rows planted or bushels harvested; the horizontal axis is the number of workers. At some point, the added worker will accomplish less than the previous worker added to the crew.

Point of Diminishing Returns

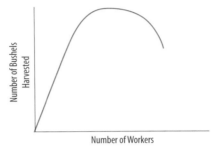

Number of Workers

This also applies to certain things in our personal lives. Think about it. We enjoy hearing a new song by our favorite band for the first time. Each successive time we hear it we like it more and more—until we start to get tired of it. But long before we're tired of it, we start to enjoy it less than we did the previous time we heard it. The very first time that occurs is the point of diminishing returns.

Formally, the law of diminishing returns states that at a certain point the marginal return—that is, the incremental return—produced by any resource will decrease with each additional unit of that resource. In other words, once you reach the point of diminishing returns, the returns keep diminishing.

Diminishing returns are an inevitable fact of life. The difficulty in business is knowing at what point returns will diminish. When should you stop additional advertising? When should you stop adding workers to a project? When have you spent enough money on market research? Generally, the answer is at the point of diminishing returns. In plain English, it's just not worth it to add more of that resource or do more of the activity.

Why the Big Get Bigger: Economies of Scale

Economies of scale explain why big companies tend to get bigger. The term refers to the fact that the average cost of making a unit of product decreases with each additional one you make. Why does this happen? Because the fixed costs are spread out over a larger number of units. The more you produce, the lower the fixed cost per unit becomes.

Let's go back to the copy shop example. Let's say the owner has a high-volume copier that costs $10,000 per year to lease. Let's also say that the variable costs—for paper and toner and so on—are 2 cents per copy.

Here's the cost per copy at 500,000 copies and at 1,000,000 copies over five years.

500,000	1,000,000
COPIES/YR	**COPIES/YR**
Total variable costs (paper, toner)	
$10,000	$20,000
Total fixed costs (annual copier lease)	
10,000	10,000

Total cost of copies

20,000	30,000

Cost per copy

$0.04	$0.03

As the table shows, though the fixed costs (the $10,000 annual cost of leasing the copier) and variable costs (2 cents per copy) are the same, the total cost per copy is lower at the higher volume. The more you produce, the greater the scale of your operation and the more economically it can do it.

Decision Trees

A decision tree is a decision-making tool that helps you assign a probability to an estimate. For example, let's say a pizzeria owner has an opportunity to expand to the west side of his own city or into the next city. Or he could choose not to expand at all. Let's say that he estimates his profits over the next five years at each of the two potential locations to be:

Estimate	West Side	Next City
OPTIMISTIC	6 million	5 million
BEST GUESS	3 million	4 million
PESSIMISTIC	2 million	2 million

Finally, let's say that for both locations, he sees a 60 percent likelihood that the best guess will occur, and a 20 percent likelihood that either the optimistic or pessimistic estimate will occur. In this case the decision tree would look like the one below:

The decision tree lets you consider alternatives and risk. Putting probabilities on the estimates forces you to think about what might really happen. When viewing an opportunity, it's easy for many of us to get carried away with optimism, so it's good to incorporate a pessimistic estimate into the analysis. The decision tree is one way of doing that.

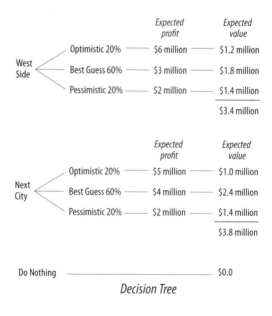

			Expected profit		Expected value
	Optimistic 20%	—	$6 million	—	$1.2 million
West Side	Best Guess 60%	—	$3 million	—	$1.8 million
	Pessimistic 20%	—	$2 million	—	$1.4 million
					$3.4 million

			Expected profit		Expected value
	Optimistic 20%	—	$5 million	—	$1.0 million
Next City	Best Guess 60%	—	$4 million	—	$2.4 million
	Pessimistic 20%	—	$2 million	—	$1.4 million
					$3.8 million

| Do Nothing | | | | | $0.0 |

Decision Tree

So, what should the pizzeria owner do? If he were to make his choice strictly on the basis of the decision tree, he should choose the alternative with the highest "expected value." In our example, that means he would choose to expand into the next city. The expected value of that choice is $3.8 million dollars, while that of expanding to the west side is $3.4 million.

In practice, of course, he and anyone else in their right mind would use the decision tree as one tool in the analysis.

" IT'S MANAGEMENT'S JOB TO ESTABLISH PROCESSES IN WHICH ORDINARY PEOPLE CAN **ACHIEVE EXTRAORDI-NARY** RESULTS. "

—Peter F. Drucker
(author and management consultant)

8 Delivering Quality and Value

An organization exists to create a specific result, which people will pay it to deliver. By extension, each activity and project within an organization aims—or at least should aim—to create and deliver a result.

From the execution standpoint, managers and entrepreneurs exist not only to organize the factors of production, but also to manage them to produce the intended results, achieve the targeted goals, and fulfill the organization's purpose. This means establishing processes that get results, achieve goals, and fulfill purposes.

This chapter shows you how to think about, create, and manage processes that do these things. Some of these ideas are fairly sophisticated, but I've simplified them and shown how they apply to virtually any activity or project.

> **proc•ess**
>
> 1. set of linked activities organized to create a certain result
>
> 2. context in which an activity or job is performed

Characteristics of a Process

A process has several characteristics. (This material refers mainly to organizational processes but also applies in part to others, such as educational, biological, and legal processes.)

Defined steps or events: A process consists of defined steps, events, roles, and activities. For instance, a sales process consists of the methods a company uses to find, win, and keep customers.

Design: A business process has been designed and arranged by management. A process results from decisions that management has made—or failed to make.

Alignment: A process aligns activities and resources toward a common end. Managers, particularly in large organizations, often discuss alignment because they know that people often work at cross purposes. Creating alignment isn't easy, but it's a major management responsibility.

Measurements: A process and its results can be measured for quality, timeliness, cost, and profitability. To get the right results, managers must know what to measure, how to measure it, and how to analyze and evaluate the measurements.

Results: As noted, a process exists to create a result. However, not all processes produce the intended result. The job of a manager or entrepreneur is to know what's working and what isn't, and to foster more of the former while eliminating the latter. That means learning what results are being created and why.

Seeing Business Processes Clearly

Much of this chapter deals with an approach to management called process improvement. If you're not familiar with it, you may be surprised at how clearly it enables you to see what's going on in a business situation. In other words, if you view a business situation as a process that must be executed properly, you can more readily understand what's wrong and how to fix it.

I'll start with a simple tool called a SIPOC (sy-pock) diagram. SIPOC stands for Supplier, Inputs, Process, Outputs, Customer. Those are the basic elements of any business process. Get those elements right, and the execution should go right.

Essentially, the SIPOC can be used to describe almost any function, activity, or job. Here's a SIPOC for an accounting department:

Use a SIPOC to Set Things Up

The SIPOC can help you set up a job or function from scratch. Suppose you're about to hire a marketing person. What exactly is their job? You can't just say, "marketing." What input will they work on? Where will it come from? What will they do and how? What output will they produce? Who will use it and for what? Get these questions answered beforehand.

Supplier >	Inputs >	Process >	Outputs >	Customer
Purchasing, sales, and other departments	Hard copy and electronic data on transactions	Record the transactions in proper accounts	Financial reports	CEO, CFO, and other managers

You can construct a SIPOC for virtually any organization, function, or job. Here are a few more points about the SIPOC:

- *The diagram becomes complicated for large processes—say, a car manufacturer—but then you break down large processes into sub-processes and diagram those in individual SIPOCs.*

- *We usually think of a supplier and customer as being outside the company, but either or both parties can be inside, as in the case of the accounting department.*

- *Similarly, inputs may be sent outside for processing by an external outfit, then come back to be processed further or sold. A book publisher sends electronic files to a printer who prints and binds the books and ships them to the publisher's warehouses or to distributors.*

- *With a series of SIPOCs you can see that one function's or job's output is another's*

*input. You can see how activities and
results in a project or process fit together.*

Using a SIPOC

With a SIPOC, you can locate problems and see
how to fix them or even how to improve a process
that's already working well. Here are questions to ask
about each element:

Suppliers: Have we clearly communicated our
needs to suppliers? Is the supplier performing as
agreed? If not, why not?

Inputs: Are the inputs of the right type and quality? Are they arriving when and how they should?
Is there a problem in packaging, transporting, or
storing them?

Process: Is the process for converting the inputs
to outputs defined in writing? Is it being followed?
What skills and training do the workers require?
What are the steps, costs, times, and other aspects
of the process?

Outputs: Are there written standards for the quality and timeliness of outputs? What happens when
the standards are not met?

Customers: How satisfied are customers with the
quality, quantity, and timeliness of the output?
How do we know? Do customers have an easy way
to register complaints?

You could come up with questions of your own, and of course every situation will suggest its own queries. The point is that by looking at the parts of the problem, rather than jumping to conclusions, you will come up with better solutions.

The SIPOC is only one tool of process improvement, which is not just an approach to management, but an entire movement.

Learn to Lean a Little

Lean is a method for getting the entire company aligned toward creating value for the customer. Now, I realize that "value for the customer" has become a cliché, but that doesn't mean that customers don't want value. As with most difficult things, delivering value to the customer is something that some people talk about and others work at.

There are five basic principles in Lean:

1. Value: This means identifying what customers do and don't value, and doing more of the former and less of the latter. For example, if customers don't care what color your product comes in, just make it black or white instead of designing, producing, carrying, selling, and delivering a dozen different colors. If they value more power or reliability, put resources into making the product more powerful or reliable.

2. Value stream: You analyze the value stream by identifying the process by which the product is created or the service is delivered to the customer. The SIPOC diagram can come in handy here. If you can identify the suppliers, inputs, processes, outputs, and customers at every point in the stream, you can improve it.

3. Flow: You make the value stream flow more quickly by eliminating anything that you do that the customer doesn't value. Making twelve colors when customers want one or two is a good example again. Stop dealing with all the colors, and the process will flow faster.

4. Pull: A Lean process lets customers pull the product—that is, order it and take delivery when they need it—rather than forcing them to carry large inventories. Just-in-time manufacturing grew out of Lean. Indeed, the entire music downloading phenomenon allows customers to pull product rather than have stores carry inventory—and lets customers buy only what they want.

5. Perfection: Lean says that an organization, individual, or area

> **just-in-time man•u•fac •tur•ing**
>
> 1. process that delivers materials to workers when they need them
>
> 2. process that delivers small quantities to customers when ordered or on schedule

should constantly strive to reach perfection. This is the famous goal of zero errors, and it is virtually impossible to achieve. Yet striving toward perfection will minimize errors to the point at which they can become negligible.

What's a Six Sigma?

Six Sigma is a fraternity at University of Miami where they—just kidding. Six Sigma actually means several things. First, it is a statistical term for a measure of quality that means 3.4 defects per million chances for a defect. For instance, that translates to a little more than three bottles of beer, boxes of cornflakes, or cans of soup being spoiled, short in weight or volume, or leaky per million bottles, boxes, or cans.

Take Action
For a highly readable overview of Six Sigma, get ahold of *The Six Sigma Way* by Peter S. Pande, Robert P. Neuman, and Roland R. Cavanagh (McGraw-Hill, 2000).

That's a high level of quality, and it is attainable for packaged goods such as food, paper towels, and toothpaste. It's when products contain moving parts or face rough use that such quality becomes almost unattainable. In services, it depends on how automated the process is. ATMs execute at high levels of accuracy, but tellers and clerks are human beings subject to distraction, fatigue, and daydreams.

More broadly, Six Sigma is an approach to managing a process so that it produces the intended result. Some people use the term loosely, to mean almost any fact-based management approach. But formally it is a five-step approach to solving problems and improving quality.

A Five-Step Solution

As a formal approach, Six Sigma consists of five steps—Define, Measure, Analyze, Improve, Control—commonly called DMAIC (da may' ik). Let's look at each of these steps briefly.

Define: Define means define the problem as accurately as possible. You can't define the problem as "that bozo running the Atlanta office." Rather, you define the problem in terms of the results the process is producing, such as "Employee turnover has doubled in the past year." You might have to go through several iterations to define the problem and then that becomes the problem to be addressed.

> **THE FIVE STEPS OF SIX SIGMA**
>
> o Define
>
> o Measure
>
> o Analyze
>
> o Improve
>
> o Control

Measure: One key to process improvement is to measure the results and the activities of the process before and after you try to improve them. That way you'll know whether and by how much you succeeded. Equally important, measuring activities and results tells you where resources are being allocated and what returns they are generating.

Analyze: Data and measurements will sometimes pinpoint the problem right away, but usually you must analyze them to identify waste, errors, and bottlenecks. Six Sigma includes many tools for analyzing data, including sophisticated statistical methods. However, it also includes simple, non-technical tools as well (such as the SIPOC diagram). Regardless of how it's conducted, the analyze step aims to identify the cause of defects and errors, so that cause can be eliminated and the process improved.

Improve: This is the step where you first choose and then implement a solution to the problem. In strict Six Sigma, you approach the improve step as an experiment. Your hypothesis is that X (an element in the process) is the cause of Y (the error or defect) and that if you eliminate X you will eliminate Y. In practice, managers often just see the solution and implement it. Yet when the solution could be complicated or expensive, manag-

pi•lot pro•ject

1. small-scale implementation of a large-scale project to test effectiveness

2. means of testing methods and solutions at relatively low cost

ers will conduct a pilot project to see if it works before committing major resources to it. Once you learn the solution, you write it up as the new policy or procedure and ensure that the relevant people can carry it out.

Control: The control step is the ongoing management task of ensuring that the new policies and procedures are being implemented and that they work. Certain measures of quality, productivity, timeliness, or customer satisfaction must be in place so managers will know if things go out of whack again. If they do, the situation must be reexamined to determine whether the original solution failed or a new condition has come up.

Using Process Improvement

Lean and Six Sigma represent highly sophisticated management approaches. They have been widely accepted and practiced in major companies, mainly in production areas but also in marketing, sales, and finance. I personally have found that just knowing how a process approach works helps me to be more efficient and effective even though I work mainly on book projects.

For a broader application, let's return to our example of the copy shop in Chapter 7 and see how Six Sigma might help its owner solve problems.

Suppose the owner now runs four copy shops. He has grown by landing commercial accounts from mid-sized businesses that need reports copied and bound when they can't handle the volume internally. But after winning more business and adding a commercial account executive and a production manager at his two largest stores, he's now seeing more complaints from customers. This is generating jobs that have to be run twice, which cuts into his profits, and he's even lost two large accounts due to (he suspects) quality problems. He's also seeing more complaints about jobs being delivered late. What should he do?

Obviously, he should talk to his account executive and production manager. But unless they have good data at hand, the owner will probably hear imprecise reports, along with explanations and excuses that may or may not be valid. But with a process-oriented approach, he would:

Define the problem by examining the work orders, due dates, and invoices for the jobs customers weren't happy with, then talking to some or all of the large customers to learn about their expectations and how the copy shop failed to meet them. The problem might be tardiness, rework, poor quality, or some combination of these, but usually one key problem—such as poor quality at one store or at a certain time or when certain operators are on—would emerge.

Measure the activities and results by adding up the time that the original runs and rework took, the cost of rework, and the profits lost. Also review the specifications, calibrations, maintenance records, and operating procedures for the machines to see if all are correct and being followed. Then determine how operators are setting up jobs, getting customer approval on samples, and running the machines.

Analyze the situation by seeing if the machines are properly calibrated, regularly maintained, and capable of this volume, and that the correct paper, toner, and bindings are being used. Observe operators and machines in action. Determine if the problem resides in the machines, operating procedures, materials, or interaction with customers.

Improve the process by correcting the problem and putting proper procedures in place, reviewing them carefully with staff as needed. If necessary, work with the account executive regarding customer expectations and how to resolve problems with large jobs, and work with the store manager regarding the machinery, materials, and operators.

Control the process going forward by closely monitoring large jobs and customer satisfaction on a regular basis. Avoid backsliding by instituting a weekly or monthly review of the data that indicated the problem so that the process does not deteriorate.

" MARKETING IS **NOT AN EVENT, BUT A PROCESS. . . .** IT HAS A BEGINNING, A MIDDLE, BUT NEVER AN END, FOR IT IS A PROCESS. YOU IMPROVE IT, PERFECT IT, CHANGE IT, EVEN PAUSE IT. BUT YOU NEVER STOP IT COMPLETELY. "

—Jay Conrad Levinson
(author)

9 Executing Marketing Plans

In today's marketplace, it has become almost impossible for an organization to succeed without superb marketing efforts.

Well-executed marketing plans begin with a quality product or service—one that does what it's supposed to and delivers the expected benefits. It then goes on to target the best customers, create compelling messages, and deliver them via the right media.

This chapter shows how to go about planning and executing a marketing effort. Given that thousands of books have been written on the subject, what can this chapter offer? It clearly presents the three key elements in marketing—that is, targeting, messaging, and media—and shows how they fit together and work together in the planning and execution stages.

Marketing in a Nutshell

In my research for this book I came across one of the best summaries I've seen of the major tools of marketing. I wish I could tell you who wrote it, but I found it attributed to an unknown individual at a site called MuseumMarketingTips.com, which helps museums, zoos, and similar nonprofits market themselves:

If the circus is coming to town and you paint a sign saying "Circus Coming to the Fairground Saturday," that's advertising. If you put the sign on the back of an elephant and walk it into town, that's promotion. If the elephant walks through the mayor's flower bed, that's publicity. And if you get the mayor to laugh about it, that's public relations. If the town's citizens go the circus, you show them the entertainment booths, explain how much fun they'll have at the booths, answer their questions and ultimately, they spend a lot at the circus, that's sales.

I'll elaborate just a bit on this:

Advertising is paying a media outlet to carry your message to an audience. It may be broadcast, cable, or satellite media, Web-based media, print media, or even space on billboards or public transit vehicles.

Promotion is more loosely defined but mainly includes devices and offers that get your product, service, or organization noticed by potential customers. Companies use promotional items such as coffee mugs, calendars, and pens to create awareness. Businesses run special offers, such as two-for-one or time-limited discounts as promotions to boost awareness, and if possible, purchases.

Publicity is also defined somewhat loosely, but usually means efforts to create public awareness by sponsoring events, such as foot races, NASCAR vehicles, concerts, or trade shows. Some people use the term to mean public relations.

Public relations (or PR) can overlap conceptually with publicity—as in, "It's good public relations to sponsor charity events"—but specifically refers to efforts to generate media interest in your company, products, or services. It's positive coverage that you don't pay the newspaper, magazine, or media outlet for, although you can pay a public relations firm to help you get that coverage.

Selling, again, usually means one-to-one efforts to persuade someone to buy your product or service. Selling has become quite sophisticated and focuses more on addressing customers' needs than on pressuring them into buying. Also, although

Take Action
For good information on the persuasive aspects of selling, see the book on *Persuasion* in this Adams Media series.

most forms of direct marketing, such as direct mail and telemarketing, are called "marketing," they are really selling. They're called marketing because they are efforts to sell to groups, but if they ask for an order, that's selling.

Targeting the Right Customers

In planning a marketing program, you start by matching the product and the customer. Actually, that starts in the product development stage, which means you must focus on the customer's needs right from the start. If your product or service does not meet a true customer need, you're in trouble.

However, some customers have a greater need than others and thus will be more likely to buy. Those are usually the customers you want to target first. As I explained in the book on *Innovation* in this Adams Media series, in every market for a new technology there are Innovators (3 percent of the total market), Early Adopters (13 percent), Early Majority (34 percent), Late Majority (34 percent), and Laggards (16 percent). If you're selling a truly new product you must target the Innovators and Early Adopters for that type of product.

But what if you're not selling something really new? By really new, I mean really new, in the way that the personal computer, the cell phone, and the Segue personal transportation device were new. I don't mean in the ways that a new line of jeans, breakfast cereal, or resorts are new.

The task of targeting the right market is unique to the product or service, so there are few guidelines I can offer. But those guidelines are key to the success of your marketing effort.

How to Target Your Markets

As you may know, the two major markets are consumers, on the one hand, and, on the other, businesses (and other organizations). Consumers are people who purchase products and services for their own use. Businesses also consist of people, but people who purchase products and services for use by their organizations. The latter market is called the business-to-business market, or B-to-B (or B2B) market.

Trying to characterize marketing by the product or service can be deceptive. For instance there are true consumer products, like cornflakes and cigarettes, and there are true business products, like earthmoving equipment. But there are many gray areas. I know people who buy only Apple computers for their homes, but PCs for their businesses. The rise of the home-based business has made the office supplies category a bifurcated market of businesses and consumers.

In any event, targeting markets goes well beyond figuring out whether you're after consumers or businesses. Indeed, you also have to segment and prioritize your customers. In segmenting, you classify your customers by certain characteristics. In prioritizing, you assess the segments in terms of need for your product, likelihood of purchase, potential profitability (to you), and other characteristics, and then rank their attractiveness.

Segmenting: Divvy Them Up

To segment a market you classify customers so you can group them, consider their needs and attitudes, and market to them in useful ways. Market segments

141

psy•cho •graph•ics

1. study of the psychological and lifestyle character- istics of consumers

2. considers factors such as politics, hobbies, vacation preferences, and attitudes

dem•o• graph•ics

1. study of con- sumers' age, income, and edu- cational level, and family factors such as marital status and number of children

2. more factual than psychograph- ics, but not geared toward assessing attitudes such as political leanings or environmental consciousness

exist for virtually every group of potential customers for every type of product. In both consumer and B-to-B markets, you have various ways to segment your markets on characteristics such as:

Size
Age
Income or profitability
Location
Lifestyle or profile

However you go about it, you must segment your market so that you can plan your marketing approaches.

Prioritize Your Market Segments

Once you have segmented your customers, you can classify them—and any new ones who come along—into those seg- ments. Wealthy consumers go into the wealthy consumer data- base, small retailers go into the small retailer database, and so on. But as you plan your market- ing efforts, which categories will be most receptive to which messages and the most attractive to you as customers?

How I Did It

When I set out to ghostwrite business books, I targeted consultants with at least $1 million in annual sales at business addresses in greater Boston. Most consultants want a book to showcase their expertise and have material for a book. Those with $1 million in revenue and an office could probably afford my fee. However, the greater Boston part was unimportant; I've written books for clients in California, Florida, and Georgia.

Answering these questions calls for serious thinking. For instance, when I started ghostwriting business books, some friends of mine thought I should approach large consulting firms. However, while they have large budgets, they are also harder to sell to because the decision makers are difficult to reach and large firms usually make decisions by committee. By targeting smaller firms, I found it easy to reach the decision makers and get a yes or no.

Two excellent ways to prioritize your customers are by their usage of your product or their perceived need, which typically affect their likelihood of purchase. Given the difficulty of marketing/selling it's best to first approach customers who are most likely to buy.

Another good way of prioritizing customers is by the likely size of order. You may initially think the bigger, the better, but be careful. If you're starting out, it's often preferable to target smaller customers first so you can refine your approach and see the product in action—and ramp up operations to handle more volume—before approaching the big ones.

Again, however you go about it, you must prioritize your market segments so you can budget your marketing and sales money wisely and put first things first. Once you have your markets segmented and prioritized, you must craft compelling sales messages.

> In marketing I've seen only one strategy that can't miss—and that is to market to your best customers first, your best prospects second, and the rest of the world last.
> —John Romero (casino marketing consultant)

Massage the Message

In this chapter, marketing includes all efforts used to send messages to groups. By messages I mean communications designed to position your product, service, brand, or organization in the minds of your market or audience. Your goal should be to have them respond in some way, by buying your product, making a donation, asking for more information, or taking some other action step.

Be sure you understand which benefits are most compelling to your audience. This means understanding your customers deeply. For instance, the idea of saving money actually doesn't appeal to everyone. Some people enjoy paying more because they believe it ensures higher quality, better service, or greater expertise. (Let me put it this way: Do you want the cheapest surgeon in your area?)

Understanding customers means getting to know them. Talk with them in both structured and unstructured ways. Structured ways take the form of market research, in which you use a well-designed survey questionnaire to get the answer to specific questions. Unstructured talks occur during sales calls on the phone or in person, in customer service situations, and when you receive complaints. However, the results of those unstructured talks should be captured in a systematic way and then put into some kind of structured form.

Take Action
Check out *High Visibility: Transforming Your Personal and Professional Brand* by Irving Rein, Philip Kotler, Michael Hamlin, and Martin Stoller (McGraw-Hill, third edition, 2005).

Media: Use a Mix

Many businesses, especially small ones, make the mistake of using only one or two media to get their marketing message out. If one or two media work for you, that's fine. It does happen, especially for a one-person shop. But usually even small businesses benefit by launching multiple efforts to get their messages out.

I use "media" here in the broadest sense of the term. Clearly, a small business or professional firm does not sit around trying to figure out how much of their media budget to place with the television networks and how much to put into major magazines. That's for major consumer products outfits with huge advertising budgets.

But even small companies can use a mix of media. Consider the following as elements in the mix for

145

a small firm of consultants, attorneys, or financial planners:

- *Direct mail*
- *Web sites*
- *Public relations*
- *Speaking engagements*
- *Advertising*

Getting your target markets, messages, and media right can take time. Some products, markets, and companies nail them from the start, but many take time to find their markets and the right messages and media mix. Build that time into your planning, and to the extent possible keep your operation small and marketing expenditures low until you have the winning combination.

To win business you have to ask for it. After you pave the way with sound marketing, use selling skills to learn about specific customer's needs and to show how you can meet those needs for the business.

MARKETING MISTAKES

- *Overspending before knowing what works*
- *Unprofessional execution*
- *Giving up too soon*
- *Failure to sell after marketing*

MANAGING GROWTH, SETBACKS, AND SUCCESS

part

3

" IT WAS OUR DUTY TO EXPAND. THOSE WHO CANNOT OR WILL NOT JOIN US ARE TO BE PITIED. **WHAT WE WANT TO DO, WE CAN DO** AND WILL DO, TOGETHER. "

—Ingvar Kamprad
(founder, IKEA)

10 Growing a Business

The various functions, activities, processes, and tasks of an organization—or of an individual effort—come together in the execution of a business plan. (I'm using the term business plan here to mean an overall plan for a business, nonprofit, or project.) It's a juggling act in which you, as manager or entrepreneur, must constantly decide how to allocate your time, money, people, and other resources given changing conditions and priorities.

It's impossible to follow a plan slavishly, even if you want to, because conditions and priorities will inevitably change. I cover troubleshooting and addressing crises in the next chapter. This chapter deals with achieving growth, largely by means of sound financial management. Part of that is dealing with financial problems, so I cover recognizing and solving them in this chapter as well.

Everyone Needs to Grow

Everyone in an organization, as well as anyone who's self-employed, must focus on ways to grow their business. This applies to managers of functional areas within a larger company as well. Suppose you manage the in-house print and copy shop for your company. You may think you don't have to worry about marketing and sales, because your area is basically a cost center.

Well, think again. Think back to the SIPOC diagram, which I covered in Chapter 8. You have internal customers—the "C" in SIPOC. Which internal departments use your department the most? Which ones don't use you? How satisfied are those that use your shop? How do those that don't use you get their printing and copying done? Don't you want to have more of the organization using your services? What sort of outside competitors do you face? Remember, your company could always decide to outsource your function to a local copy shop or a chain.

So a growth strategy ensures that you always have customers, and, hopefully, a job. Of course if you run your own business or have (or want) significant responsibility within your organization, you must understand how an organization grows.

Getting off to a Fast Start

A plan must be clear, aggressive but realistic, and agreed upon by all key members of the team. The team must also commit to getting off to a very fast start. They must put the plan into action quickly and vigorously, especially when it comes to marketing and sales efforts. Getting off to a fast start means bringing in business quickly, and if it's not happening you have to quickly figure out why.

If your organization is not growing, you probably have a problem with marketing, sales, pricing, or your product. To determine which kind of problem you have, you must listen very carefully to what your prospects and customers are telling you. If they won't talk to you, can't understand your product, or don't trust you, you probably have a marketing or sales problem. If they will talk to you and seem interested in the product but always balk at the price, your price is probably too high for the perceived value. (Similarly, if you're selling a lot but not making much of a profit, your price may be too low.) If they buy the product, but have problems using it, want to return it, or fail to realize the promised benefits, then you have a product problem, perhaps with quality, installation, or customer training.

Take Action

For a wealth of information on managing a small business, visit the Small Business Administration Web site at *www.sba.gov*.

These problems can overlap or become intertwined. In any event, you must properly diagnose the problem and then adjust or fix your marketing, sales, pricing, product, or performance. If you are just starting out, the best approach is to not place big bets on anything until you have used smaller experiments to see what works.

Growing Too Slow or Too Fast

No matter how well a business has been planned, things rarely proceed according to plan. After a business starts up or when an established business implements a new growth strategy, the entrepreneurs or managers generally face one of two problems—growing too slowly or growing too quickly.

IF GROWTH IS TOO SLOW

○ Evaluate your marketing plan and sales process

○ Learn whether you are delivering on promises

○ Get the necessary resources in place

A Tortoise in Its Shell?

If the business is growing too slowly, consider the following steps:

Examine your marketing plan. Pay special attention to your markets, messages, and media to see where you may have gone wrong.

Evaluate your sales process. If you're not generating interest, seeing enough prospects, getting positive feedback, or closing enough sales, where in that sequence is the problem?

Apply a process approach (as outlined in Chapter 8) to look for causes and effects. Use measures to characterize your prospects and customers, and to understand how much you are spending on which marketing and sales activities, and which of those yields the best results. Then adjust your activities accordingly.

Learn whether you are delivering as promised. Serious sales efforts must be backed up by first-rate products and service.

Obtain the resources you need to grow the business. For instance, if you are off to a slow start because you lack money, people, equipment, or other resources, do what you can to get them—on a gradual, low-cost, or contingency basis.

Often, patience and persistence will see you through a slow start or a slowdown. But you have to know why things are slow and, if possible, fix the situation. If it's a temporary condition caused by external events, you can probably ride it out. If it's something you're doing wrong, or you were too optimistic, you can correct that. But, if the problem is structural rather than temporary then you have another situation on your hands, which I'll discuss later in this chapter.

A Tiger by the Tail

When a business is growing too quickly, you have a different kind of problem. Yes, we should

---

struc•tur•al prob•lem

1. defect rooted in your marketplace, business model, or basic assumptions

2. problem that will persist unless the underlying structural issue can be addressed

---

> Today many compa-
> nies are reporting
> that their number one
> constraint on growth
> is their inability to
> hire workers with the
> necessary skills.
> —Bill Clinton (U.S.
> president)

all have such problems, yet a rap-idly growing company can soon find itself undermining its own success.

If the business is growing too fast, again try to figure out why. In fact, let's first define what "too fast" means. Too fast means that custom-ers want products and services faster than you can make and deliver them. (This is usually a good time to increase your prices.) Too fast means you can't get enough employees, or get enough of what you need from suppliers, to meet demand. Too fast means that customers are complaining, defecting, return-ing goods, or demanding refunds.

Depending on the results of your analysis, try one or more of the following:

- *Exercise leadership to motivate people through the long hours and high demands that growth imposes on a company. But leadership alone is not enough. Be certain your people share in the rewards of growth through higher salaries, bonuses, or profit sharing.*

- *Do whatever you can to maintain high quality as you grow. When problems do arise, fix them fast even if it costs you money. You don't want disappointed*

154

customers spreading the news that you don't have your act together.

- *Avoid taking on major fixed costs until you know your business has permanently expanded. If you're strapped for resources, outsource some production or service functions wholly or partly. That way, you temporarily increase your variable costs instead of permanently increasing your fixed costs.*

- *If you have investors, keep them informed of your success and problems. They may well be willing to invest additional money in a growing business, and you can finance expansion that way. However, investment should ideally be used to finance fixed assets or activities that you know will result in a permanently higher level of business.*

- *As a business grows, it typically needs to be professionalized in ways that a small business can get along without. For instance, you may need a "real" operating manager or CEO, may find yourself subject to regulations that don't apply to smaller outfits, and may require new financial controls and procedures—as well as a chief accountant or an accounting firm rather than a bookkeeper.*

Achieving Profitable Growth

To grow profitably, a company must increase sales while controlling—or even cutting—costs. The five basic strategies for increasing sales are to:

1. Sell more existing products and services to existing customers.
2. Sell more existing products and services to new customers.
3. Sell new products and services to existing customers.
4. Sell new products and services to new customers.
5. Raise prices, either across the board or on certain products and services.

Executing these strategies means focusing marketing and operational plans on those objectives and putting the resources and processes in place to support them. Each functional area and person in the organization must understand the strategy and be working toward it. Two or even three of these strategies can be pursued simultaneously, but in that case they should be prioritized. The more focused you are on a strategy, the more likely it is to succeed.

Watch the Pipeline

As you pursue a growth strategy, pay close attention to the sales pipeline. Many businesses are characterized by a sales cycle measured in days, weeks, or months. The sales pipeline consists of prospects in various stages of the sales cycle. You can forecast near-term sales by examining the number of potential customers in that pipeline, talking with your salespeople (or yourself, if you do the selling) about the chances of closing individual sales in the near future, and estimating the sales revenue for forthcoming periods accordingly.

It is, however, easy for salespeople to overestimate the amount of business that will close, so be realistic when you assess the pipeline. Look at the number of customers, the size of the likely orders, and the ones or the percentage you will close based on experience. Never count on business that you're not sure about.

sales cy•cle

1. average amount of time it takes for a company to sell to a customer

2. varies widely among industries, and is watched most closely in B-to-B sales

Monitor cash flow, but understand the difference between cash flow problems and structural financial problems. Cash flow problems are problems of timing, in which outgo precedes income. The problem isn't that you don't have the money, but that you don't have the money yet. You can usually solve cash flow problems by borrowing short-term and paying it back when you collect the income. In contrast, structural problems reside in your cost or price structure or in your business model, and you shouldn't confuse them with temporary cash flow problems.

Look Down the Road

In B-to-B sales, if you want early warning signs of financial trouble, try to monitor your customers' customers. You do this by talking with your customers and learning about their business, their products and services, and their concerns about their customers. In retail sales, watch interest rates, housing starts, and local and regional unemployment—all of which are regularly reported in the news.

Boosting Sales

Managers often see sales slide, or learn that their forecast was too optimistic, and fail to respond quickly. If sales are lower than expected, you can adjust the forecast (which is like retouching your x-rays) or you can work to boost sales.

Most managers tend to push the sales force harder in an effort to increase sales. They harangue them to make more sales calls and to bring in business. But when sales are off, it's usually not because the salespeople are loafing. It's usually because something about customers' needs or marketplace dynamics has changed. This could feed back to your product or pricing, either or both of which may no longer be competitive.

It's management's job to figure out what the real sales problem is and to solve it. This calls for applying a process approach or fixing your marketing, sales, product, or pricing, or perhaps troubleshooting as discussed in Chapter 11. If, however, the problem cannot be solved quickly—or even if it can—you must take action to boost near-term sales with potentially useful measures including the following:

- *Offer limited-time discounts and special offers.*

- *Launch a quick, low-cost marketing program to former customers, dormant accounts, and customers who now buy less from you.*

- *Look at your products or services and see if, given their configuration, there's an opportunity to bundle or un-bundle them to encourage sales.*

- *Urge salespeople to focus on selling the most profitable products or on selling to the most profitable customers.*

- *Provide special incentives to salespeople (the lower the cost, the better).*

TO BOOST SHORT-TERM SALES

- *Offer limited-time discounts.*

- *Focus on former or dormant customers.*

- *Reconfigure your offerings.*

- *Give salespeople new incentives.*

Take Action
For an excellent guide to managing growth profitably, get a copy of *Profit Building: Cutting Costs Without Cutting People* by Perry J. Ludy (Berrett-Koehler, 2000).

Money Problems

If profitable growth does not materialize, sooner or later financial problems will. If people—particularly people in key positions—are not executing as planned, if sales are not growing, and if costs are not well controlled, money problems will arise. If they do arise, two things will help you solve them: early detection and rapid response.

Early detection calls for closely monitoring monthly (or, better still, weekly) reports on variances in sales and expense budgets, which I discussed in Chapter 6. Look for large variances in either absolute or percentage amounts, especially overspending, but also underspending, and, second, look for trends of over- or underspending over several weeks or months.

Rapid response means addressing the causes of low sales, as discussed earlier in this chapter, and spending variances. Because a budget is a plan and a forecast—in other words, a set of estimates—you'll typically find a mix of overspending and underspending. Here are ways to get costs under control.

ab•so•lute and per•cent•age

1. absolute amounts are the actual figures in currency, such as $1,000 overspending on a $10,000 budget item

2. percentage amounts are the percentages of the over- or underspending, such as 10 percent over on a $10,000 budget item

Getting Costs Under Control

The basic strategies for cutting costs focus on reducing fixed costs, variable costs, or both. For example, over the past two decades U.S. companies have reduced labor costs by outsourcing functions formerly performed by employees and by hiring lower-cost employees in states with fewer unionized workers and in countries with lower labor costs. Many have also, or instead, reduced fixed costs by building production facilities and offices in relatively low-cost areas of the country, such as the South and Southwest, or outside the country—and by outsourcing production to contract manufacturers.

Two other options are to reduce the growth rate of costs or to pass on increased costs to customers in the form of price increases. It can be difficult to reduce the growth of costs that are rising because of market forces, such as wages and health insurance. The

Let the Customer Do It

One common cost reduction strategy is to offload certain costs onto the customer. Many grocery stores now feature lines where you scan your purchases yourself and pay at a machine. Fast-food restaurants have customers draw their own drinks (and, often, clean their own tables). We pump our own gas and wait for long stretches on hold to speak with customer service representatives—all costs to us rather than to the companies we're doing business with.

market is bigger than all of us, which is why many manufacturers have moved production to lower-cost foreign locations. The cost of energy is also hard to control, but many companies have adopted conservation techniques such as sophisticated controls, improved maintenance, and special contracts with suppliers.

Another major challenge in cost control is to avoid eroding the quality of products and services as you cut costs. You can almost always hire cheaper labor, but can they do the job as well as someone who charges a higher rate? You can typically purchase cheaper materials, but won't customers notice the poorer performance and shorter life of your products?

Financial Warning Signs

Financial trouble usually builds slowly. Yet because most business people are optimists, or at least try to be, they often don't want to see that trouble. So they either ignore what their financial is telling them or see negative development and hope for a miracle.

To avoid financial trouble, watch for—and respond to—these warning signs:

- *Increased price resistance from customers. If customers question your pricing more intensely, they may be facing financial pressure or have a new alternative. Try to learn why they're questioning your price and review your pricing policies to ensure that they're realistic.*

- *Lower levels of sales per customer, smaller orders, and less frequent orders, especially from a customer or market segment that you depend heavily upon.*

- *Slower payments from customers. When your customers face financial pressure, they will typically pay their bills more slowly unless you are absolutely essential to their business.*

- *Higher prices for the goods and services you purchase, especially if a major supplier has increased prices.*

- *Red flags such as allowing your insurance premiums to lapse, failing to pay your estimated quarterly federal or state income taxes, financing short-term expenses with long-term liabilities, and losing good employees.*

To Address Financial Trouble

Addressing financial trouble usually means cutting costs, delaying payments, speeding up receipts, and, if things are getting tight, talking with creditors—without causing them to panic. Here are steps you can take to get costs under control:

Review expenses and then delay, reduce, or eliminate any that are not related to selling, creating, and delivering products and services. Then, if necessary, delay or reduce expenditures that are related to selling, creating, and delivering products and services, if you can do so without significantly compromising sales or quality.

Speed up collection efforts. A slowdown in sales is often tied to a downturn in business conditions. When that happens, your customers will start paying you more slowly. But they'll tend to pay suppliers that call and ask where the check is, so be among those suppliers and you'll improve your cash flow.

Renegotiate terms on loans or other money owed. Many lenders and creditors will renegotiate interest rates and payment amounts and schedules. They're not happy about doing so, but they will if it means eventually collecting rather than writing off the amount. Just make sure the new terms aren't so onerous that they do you in.

If you have to cut staff, do it sooner rather than later. Although stories of layoffs are as widespread as they are sad, many companies wait too long to lay off workers when financial trouble hits. It's difficult, but if it means the difference between the business closing down and surviving—and eventually rehiring people—then layoffs must be done.

When Good Times Fade

Many of us upgrade our business lifestyles in good times. If you do, be sure to downgrade when during bad times. Don't think of expensive restaurants, travel, cars, consultants, offices, clubs, and so on as business essentials. They probably aren't. Even if they are, you stand a better chance of survival if you retrench. Be frank with customers that you can trust; most of us have been there despite our façades.

Work hard to make it, but avoid financial— or personal—ruin. Businesses fail every day and many ultimately successful entrepreneurs have overseen the demise of an enterprise. Many ultimately successful managers have been fired. There's actually no shame attached to it, unless you engaged in fraud, embezzlement, or other forms of dishonesty. If you fail you'll have to cut back on your lifestyle and work your way back up, but once you absorb the hit—even bankruptcy—you will live to fight another day.

"

TROUBLE IS THE COMMON DENOMINA-
TOR OF LIVING. IT IS **THE GREAT
EQUALIZER**.

"

—Søren Kierkegaard
(Danish philosopher)

11

Problem Solving and Trouble- shooting

Call it Murphy's Law, the way of the world, or whatever you want, but implementing decisions and executing plans will rarely, if ever, go smoothly.

As a philosopher once said, if it's not one thing it's another. People, of course, represent a constant source of difficulty, not because they're difficult (well, some are) but because people have different motives, skills, and communication styles, which often come into conflict. And then there are crises and catastrophes that seem to appear out of nowhere.

This chapter focuses on your responses to the glitches, setbacks, and troubles that will arise on the road to a successful project or business. It's about troubleshooting as opposed to problem solving, about dealing with specific forms of trouble—most of which are people problems or project delays—and what to do if you encounter a genuine crisis.

To me, troubleshooting differs from straight-up problem solving in that it's based more on intuition and experience than on analysis of facts and figures. Why? Because facts and figures can be hard to come by when trouble descends, and you might not have the time to analyze them anyway. Also, when they are available and you have time, the facts and figures themselves are extremely unpleasant.

So, trouble will come knocking on your door. Here's what to do when you can't slide out the back.

Troubleshooting Guidelines

The basic guideline is to expect and accept glitches, setbacks, and troubles as a normal part of a process or project. This isn't pessimism, but realism. Things will rarely go according to plan, so if you expect trouble you won't go to pieces when it crops up. Here are a few more guidelines:

Face the situation squarely. You can deal with trouble only when you admit that it exists.

Respond to the first sign of trouble. Have you ever ignored a small problem, only to see it grow into a large one? Some problems do arise with little or no warning, but other kinds of trouble, especially those involving employees, start small. Respond when they're small and you'll usually be dealing with manageable problems. (Notice I said respond, not react.)

Remain calm, get perspective, get advice.
It's easy to see real trouble as the end of the world, your business, or your career. Yet that's rarely the case. So take things in stride to the extent that you can and listen to others' views and ideas.

Be honest with people, including yourself.
Two situations prompt most of us to lie to ourselves and others. When we are wrong, and when we have to tell someone that they are wrong. In these cases, lying precludes a solution because people can't deal with problems that they can't acknowledge. Honesty enables you to deal with trouble before it gets out of hand.

Okay, now let's look at specific types of trouble that will need shooting.

Assessing People Problems

People problems stem from two major causes, both of which go back to the key questions to answer in every hiring situation: Can this person do the job? Will this person do the job?

Before we get to those questions, a word of caution is in order. Many managers assume that every problem is a people problem, but as noted in Chapter 8, the problem is often the process. So, before you assume that you have a people problem, look at the way things are supposed to be done given the procedures and expectations, then look at the actual ways in which people are working and the results they're producing.

What's Expected?

Examining the way things are supposed to be done often reveals that the procedures are nonexistent, unclear, complex, or outdated. In such situations, people try to do things in the most practical way rather than by the book. They're going to ignore procedures that slow them down or fail to produce a visible benefit.

If you ask people about your expectations, you may find similar things at work. Go back to the basics of delegation: Did you clearly communicate your expectations about the results, methods, and deadline? Were your expectations reasonable, and did the person agree to them? Did you make it clear that you were available to offer advice and assistance? Did you set frequent milestones and interim deadlines?

What's Happening?

Examining what someone is doing and the results they are getting often reveals a misunderstanding of procedures or poor execution. Next time you're on a golf course or at a gym, look carefully at the people around you. You'll see that few of them properly execute the fundamentals of the golf swing or proper weight-lifting form. Given that success in any endeavor depends on diligent execution of the fundamentals, it's no wonder ponds are full of golf balls and sports injuries abound.

Don't assume that people who have, or who are supposed to have, certain skills use them to full effect. Instead, look to see what they don't understand, never learned, or fail to do correctly. Then it's a matter of coaching and correcting them.

Real people problems are not really addressable with coaching and correcting, which is all in a day's work for a manager. But people problems can be addressed.

Addressing People Problems

You think money troubles are the worst kind to have? Well, they can be, but people problems carry an emotional component that can rip you up like nothing else. For instance, the reason many managers tolerate poor performers is that it's unpleasant to issue reprimands and to fire someone. So they put it off, and hope the person will improve or quit. There are better ways.

First, be honest about the situation. By this I mean be honest with yourself, and with the person in question. If your expectations haven't been met, then they haven't been met. Review your expectations to see if they were reasonable, and review the ways in which you communicated them. If they were reasonable and communicated clearly, then you have to talk with the people involved. The conversation should contain words to the effect of, "This isn't what we agreed to, and we need to find a way to get things fixed and back on track."

Death by 1,000 Cuts

Some managers try to get poor performers to quit by reducing their status or responsibilities, excluding them from meetings and decisions, and so on. It eventually works, but it can take a while and generates negativity. It's not a pretty sight, and managers who use that approach lose the respect of some staffers. Firing people is part of the job of being a manager, so deal with it.

Seek a solution rather than blame. It's useful if the under-performer takes responsibility, but trying to get them to do so might come across as trying to blame them. Instead, appeal to their honesty and professionalism. They're probably not happy about the way things are going either, unless they are unprofessional or in a personal crisis. However, the responsibility must be on them, whether they want it or not, which is why the next question is so important.

Ask, "What is your plan?" Do not accept answers such as, "I'll just have to try harder," or "I'm going to do my best." If you get those answers, say, "That's an excellent start, but we need an actual plan at this point." Don't simply get agreement to new goals or deadlines; instead get agreement to actions that will address the situation. The person may need more help or resources. You may have to take on some of the work, or offload certain tasks to other parties. Or they may have to give you a discount so you can hire some ancillary people who can fix the situation.

Let them save face and improve their performance. If they can't come up with a plan on the spot, give them a day or two to develop one. Remember that doing more of the same won't get things back on track unless there was a one-time incident, such as a late delivery or something that had to be redone. If they come up with a plan, great. It's their plan, and they can commit to it. If they can't come up with one, work with them to develop one. If they can't or won't do that, then you probably have a terminally poor performer or an attitude case on your hands.

> " I have yet to find the man, however exalted his station, who did not do better work and put forth greater effort under a spirit of approval than under a spirit of criticism. "
> —**Charles Schwab (entrepreneur and CEO)**

Timing and Scheduling Problems

Why do so many projects fall behind schedule? There are many reasons, but two fundamental ones underlie them all. The first is lack of realism about how long things take. Why do things always take longer than we think they will, even when we know that they will take longer than we think they will (if you follow me).

There's an old question: Do you want it done fast, or do you want it done right? There's a tradeoff between speed and quality, and it's often "wished away" when people develop a timeline. Few bosses or customers enjoy hearing this question, but if they're reasonable they know this tradeoff is real. Talking about and examining how long it will take to do a good job, by looking at how long it has taken in the past, leads to more realistic schedules.

Dealing with "Scope Creep"

New requests by bosses or customers can create delays. Consultants call this phenomenon "scope creep" because new, "small" requests cause the project's scope to creep past the original parameters. I see this in my business because writing is driven by ideas, which clients never run out of. So I limit the scope of the project to three drafts and a polish, and use the phrase "That's really another book" often.

The other fundamental reason that projects fall behind schedule is the natural tension between the boss or customer and the employee or supplier. It's natural for a boss or customer to want something fast, and it's natural for an employee or supplier to want the project or the business. Put those together and you have a situation where the tension is resolved by developing an unrealistically short schedule.

However they come about, unrealistic schedules guarantee that things will fall behind. When they do, you have to take action.

Getting Projects Back on Track

To get a project back on track when it's running behind schedule, try the following:

- First, reexamine the original schedule and the process and identify what is causing the delay. Look at the CPM, PERT, and GANTT charts (covered in Chapter 3) that you used to schedule the project. Identify which tasks will be affected by those that are late. (You did use a charting tool, right?) Use a SIPOC diagram or the DMAIC approach (covered in Chapter 8) to locate the errors, waste, or bottlenecks that are causing the delays.

- Prioritize the tasks and results. You have to allocate or reallocate resources to get the project back on track, and you may need more resources. This may require a hard choice between doing some things and jettisoning some things. If it's research, can you go with a smaller sample? If it's writing, will a shorter piece work? If it's a building, can you get the next phase going early, or prefabricate parts off-site? Where can you squeeze time out of the schedule down the road?

- Reset goals and expectations with your boss, client, or supplier, or renegotiate the timetable. Can you shrink the scope of the project without undermining the original purpose? In the real world of project management, you often either have to adjust the vision of the final outcome or adjust *the schedule. If a boss or customer will not do either, they must hear that they are asking the impossible (along with an apology if you are at fault). That in itself can create new expectations.*

o *Get help. If the people you're working with can't get the job done, find people who can. This may cost more, and you may have to eat some or all of those costs, but it will solve the problem. To find the right people, hit the phones hard. In many of these situations, I've found someone who would squeeze work in for me. There is usually someone out there who wants the business, who has a hole in their schedule, who can put off another customer, or who simply wants to help a fellow human being out of a jam.*

Don't Accept Delays

Many delays occur because people accept them. When delays were unacceptable I've almost always overcome them, often with more service-oriented suppliers with the capacity to handle unexpected business. On occasion, I've also found recent U.S. immigrants more willing to give up their weekends, and more able to tap extra workers, than outfits staffed by established citizens. People hungry for business will put themselves out.

- *Get the money lined up accordingly. It may take more money to get a project back on track. Of course, the goal in execution is to bring the project in on deadline and on (or under) budget. But if you find the cause of delays and have a plan to get the project back on schedule, the choice is then between spending the money or accepting the delay. If you must eat costs, you may have to find a way to borrow money or delay payments to your suppliers without ruining yourself financially.*

Crisis Management

By crisis I mean just that—a major crisis such as a hurricane or terrorist attack, a sudden business crisis such as a large problem with a major client, or a legal or financial reversal such as the loss of a lawsuit or the arrest of a senior executive. I mean something that was either unpreventable, or something that was preventable but wasn't prevented.

One key element of crisis management is the entire matter of risk management. Almost by definition a

TO GET BACK ON SCHEDULE

- *Find the cause of delays*

- *Prioritize remaining tasks*

- *Reset goals, expectations, and deadlines*

- *Get help and, if possible, more money*

crisis comes along unexpectedly. However, while the timing of a crisis may be difficult or impossible to forecast, it is possible to anticipate the type, severity, and effects of a crisis.

When you anticipate various crises you can take measures to deal with them, to the extent possible. That way if a crisis arises, you will have basic damage control in place. Here's what I mean:

Insurance: Risk management used to focus almost solely on insurance—liability, flood, fire, and theft for businesses, and life, health, liability, and disability insurance for individuals. Risk management now extends to other areas, but insurance still stands among the basic tools.

Scenario planning: Scenario planning enables you to anticipate what would happen if various crises arose. You imagine a scenario and then anticipate the effect, often using financial and logistical models. The crisis could be natural or man-made, and scenario planning enables you to assess the likely effects of a crisis, prioritize risks, decide which risks you will assume and how you will plan for them, and develop responses.

fi•nan•cial and lo•gis•tic•al mod•els

1. mathematical equations that replicate financial and operational systems

2. tools for analyzing the potential effects of various events and various responses

Backup systems: The threat of terrorist attack, the global nature of many businesses, the dependence on information technology, and the severity of recent natural disasters have led many companies to develop backup systems, off-site recordkeeping, and contractual arrangements with private-sector disaster recovery services so they can continue operations or at least recover quickly in a crisis situation.

Take Action

For background and perspectives, see *Crisis Management: Mastering the Skills to Prevent Disasters*, a compilation of articles by various expert authors from the Harvard Business Review (Harvard Business School Press, 2004).

In the event of a crisis, first assess the situation as accurately as you can. This can be difficult. Remain calm, especially in your outward demeanor. Do not assume bad faith or incompetence or that someone is to blame. Instead, get facts about the situation by asking questions such as:

- *Who has been affected and in what ways? Has anyone been physically injured? If so, what has been done and what is being done to get them proper care?*

- *How have customers and suppliers been affected? How might they be affected? How are we communicating with them?*

- *What can we do to help? What human, physical, or financial resources can we put to work for those who have been affected?*

- *Who are the official authorities or those with the expertise to provide information and help with recovery efforts?*

Also, the following guidelines have been useful to managers facing a crisis:

Establish lines of communication and an information center or clearing house. People want and need to know what's going on. If the answer is "We don't know," then that's the answer, but it should always be followed up by, "But we're working hard to find out." Have someone—if possible, one experienced person—in charge of communications.

Make company resources available to the greatest extent practical. Many companies and managers have truly distinguished themselves by rising to the occasion during various natural and man-made disasters. Suppliers, customers, employees, and members of the public—and the media—don't forget outfits that selflessly help out during a crisis.

Get professional help if you need it. This might be legal, communications, or technical advice. Do not assume that "the law couldn't possibly mean that," or that "the supplier will have to make good on this" without verification. Don't make judgments you are not qualified to make. Instead, put off any far-reaching decisions until you get the right professional help.

> The crisis of today is the joke of tomorrow.
> —H. G. Wells (author)

Hang in There

Never abandon a cherished goal because of difficulties or setbacks. Instead, identify what's not working. Think about the cause and effect and where the shortcoming or short-circuit might be. Talk the situation over with someone you trust, especially someone more experienced and objective. And then solve the problem or overcome the troubles.

Give yourself credit for every bit of progress you make toward a goal. It's often easier to see the distance remaining between you and your goal than it is to see the distance you've already come. Keep executing as a manager, entrepreneur, or professional—and as a person—and you will achieve every goal you set and wholeheartedly pursue.